PRAISE FOR

# *Financially Capable*

"Empathetic and relatable, *Financially Capable* speaks to the heart of issues faced by young people as they make their way in a complex, confusing, and often predatory financial world."

— **DR. SARAH NEWCOMB,** Director of Financial Psychology at Morningstar and author of *Loaded: Money, Psychology, and How to Get Ahead without Leaving Your Values Behind*

"Personal finance is personal—but it's personal within a system of rules and customs. This book helps you navigate both the system and the individual choices you can make to improve your financial life."

— **ROBERT FARRINGTON,** Founder of The College Investor and Millennial Money Expert

"Matt's commitment to providing broad access to financial education and opportunities to build assets and credit has few equals. He is an excellent communicator with a gift for connecting with others."

— **PAUL HORWITZ,** former Community Affairs Specialist, FDIC

"By focusing the first two sections of his book on the financial environment and psychology, Matt Paradise's *Financially Capable* helps readers grapple with understanding why they make the decisions they do about money. He recognizes that when it comes to financial capability, that knowledge is not enough, it's understanding our own financial behaviors and the psychology behind them. An important contribution to the field!"

— **TIM RANZETTA,** Co-founder of Next Gen Personal Finance

"Matt Paradise talks about key points that the finance industry as a whole has lacked. As someone who champions financially inclusive content, *Financially Capable* touches on many of the areas that actually matter. Matt Paradise wrote a must-read book that empowers readers to question old assumptions and embrace new ideas and perspectives. This book is a helpful and actionable guide for everyone who wants to really understand what's going on with their personal finances and the financial industry."

— RAHKIM SABREE, CFEI®, RFC®,
author of *Financially Irresponsible*

"In *Financially Capable*, Matt Paradise equips his readers with a holistic array of financial information and resources. While the book focuses on the 'how-to's' of personal finance in clear, practical terms, Matt also provides the larger institutional and social contexts that intersect and impact people as they strive to meet their financial goals. Readers will be empowered to take control of their finances and futures. It is a timeless go-to guide."

— TAMMY GOOLER LOEB,
author of *Work from the Inside Out:
Break Through Nine Common Obstacles
and Design a Career That Fulfills You*

"*Financially Capable* is the guide I wish I'd had thirty years ago. When you know better, you'll do better. With this book, you'll get an educational resource that provides solid information that feels like a warm hug. Matt Paradise provides a unique perspective and valuable insight so you'll understand what to do with your money, and you'll understand why you've been thinking and behaving the way you have up until now. You'll have the tools, strategies, ideas—and most importantly, the confidence—to move into your financial future, starting today."

— HONORÉE CORDER, author of *You Must Write a Book*

"I have read my fair share of personal finance books after racking up student loan and consumer debt in my college years. However, many of the personal finance books I read assumed understanding of how capitalism, banks, and the investing economy works. I was a first-generation college student with no financial assistance from my parents. I wish I'd had a book like this one that showcases unique low- and middle-class situations that we can arise from. *Financially Capable* felt more friendly and gentle than other books I've read about slashing debt and getting rich quick. This book felt like a mentor was explaining finances to me in a compassionate, one-on-one way, and it is not riddled with judgment about past financial decisions. I also liked the character vignettes in the introduction that paint a picture of various financial scenarios that real people face."

— **SHELBY JANKE,** Technical Services Librarian, Nebraska

"Speaking from a millennial's point of view, when I started reading this book, I felt as though Matt's ideas would be a breath of fresh air to readers in my generation. I like what Matt said about how we all view wealth and finances differently and using our money to support our values and living life to the fullest will look different for different people.

"I really like the way that the book starts out. I am very interested in what Matt said about how our financial system wasn't created equally for everyone, especially across race. I also like how Matt acknowledged the emotional side of money. I feel that the way Matt organized the book to talk about these things before getting into the nuts and bolts was a great way to start the book. I have a degree in finance and love talking finance, but I also know that numbers can be very dry for some people, so leaving this part until the end was a great choice."

— **BEN BUSHART,** Staff Accountant, Los Angeles Dodgers

"Matt has such a passion for financial literacy. He has an ability to teach to diverse populations and can tailor his lessons and knowledge to any skill level. He is an absolute professional, has impeccable work ethic, and builds rapport fast."

— **ALYSON WHALEN,** Chief Operating Officer, Justice Outside

# FINANCIALLY CAPABLE

A FRIENDLY GUIDE TO

## BUILDING WHOLE-HEALTH WEALTH

## MATT PARADISE

VERNON STREET PUBLISHING

*Financially Capable: A Friendly Guide to Building Whole-Health Wealth*
by Matt Paradise © 2023

The author's goal in writing this book is to provide a source of information and empowerment for readers who desire to create healthier financial futures. The provided examples are for illustration only and names have been changed for privacy. While the publisher and author have used their best efforts in preparing this book, they make no representations or warranties regarding the accuracy or completeness of the contents of this book and disclaim any implied warranties of fitness for a particular purpose. Neither the publisher nor the author shall be liable for any loss of profit or any other commercial damages, including but not limited to special, incidental, consequential, personal, or other damages. Neither are engaged in rendering legal, tax, investment, insurance, financial, medical, or other professional advice or services. If a reader requires such advice or services, kindly consult an appropriate professional. The advice and strategies in this book and the bonuses may not be suitable for every situation.

 Published by Vernon Street Publishing
Framingham, Massachusetts
www.vernonstreetpublishing.com

Bulk order discounts are available for promotional, educational, or business use. We can create special editions with personalized covers, excerpts, and corporate imprints when you purchase in bulk. Please contact Vernon Street Publishing at SpecialMarkets@vernonstreetpublishing.com.

Publishing and Design Services: MelindaMartin.me
Proofreading by David Aretha

To schedule Matt Paradise for speaking engagements, please contact him through his website, www.MattParadise.com.

Publisher's Cataloging-in-Publication data
Names: Paradise, Matt, 1979-, author.
Title: Financially capable : a friendly guide to building whole-health wealth / Matt Paradise.
Description: Includes bibliographical references and index. | Framingham, MA: Vernon Street Publishing, 2023.
Identifiers: LCCN: 2023934614 | ISBN: 979-8-9879437-2-4 (hardcover) | 979-8-9879437-0-0 (paperback) | 979-8-9879437-1-7 (ebook)
Subjects: LCSH Finance, personal. | Investments. | Risk management. | BISAC BUSINESS & ECONOMICS / Personal Finance / Money Management | BUSINESS & ECONOMICS / Industries / Financial Services | BUSINESS & ECONOMICS / Finance / Financial Risk Management
Classification: LCC HG4529.5 .P37 2023 | DDC 332.63--dc23
ISBN 979-8-9879437-0-0 (paperback)
ISBN 979-8-9879437-1-7 (ebook)
ISBN 979-8-9879437-2-4 (hardcover)
Printed in the United States of America
First Edition
10 9 8 7 6 5 4 3 2 1

For Elsa,
my love and partner on this wild adventure;
Jayden, the next generation;
and those pursuing a rich life.

# Contents

## Part I
## FINANCIAL ENVIRONMENT
### Understanding Access and Opportunity in a Turbulent World

## Part II
## MORE THAN TOUCHY-FEELY
### The Psychology, Attitudes, Behaviors, and Emotions of Money

Part III
# NUTS AND BOLTS
## The Fundamental Knowledge of Financial Literacy

# SPECIAL INVITATION

Throughout this book are many new resources, tools, and tips on how you can become financially capable. You can also access lots of free bonus content on my website. You will find free, exclusive, never-before-published content guaranteed to enrich your journey to wealth and well-being.

To sign up for immediate access to all the resources,
visit www.MattParadise.com/capablebonus.

I'd like to invite you to connect with me:
www.linkedin.com/in/matt-paradise
TikTok @mattparadise.author

Thank you so much for your most precious resource, time, which no amount of money can buy. I look forward to hearing about your wealth building journey.

# INTRODUCTION

H ave you ever felt financial stress? If so, you're not alone. In fact, you're very much like me, your neighbors, and many others who have experienced challenges while just trying to get through life. A new study from Capital One found that 77% of Americans feel anxious about their financial situation. Under the effects of stress, people struggle to save and budget, feel less in control, and are more impulsive in how they spend their paycheck.[1]

Adulting is challenging. Financial education is useful, but knowledge is only one piece of the pie. Psychological aspects of personal finance still plague most of us. My computer is full of development courses I bought and never went through; unread books are collecting dust on shelves; and items here and there, which seemed like "must haves" but end up donated or thrown away. Let's not get started on barely used gym memberships, subscriptions for never-watched TV, and forgotten food wasting away in the fridge behind the milk.

Not so fun fact: the average American family wastes one-third of the food we buy, equaling 133 billion pounds and an estimated value of $161.6 billion. To address the problem, the US government created the 2030 Food Loss and Waste Reduction Goal. The goal seeks to cut food loss and waste in half by the year 2030.[2]

That's a lot of money being thrown away. You might be one of the few who never wastes food. Please share your secrets. The rest of us had good intentions before the spinach became slimy and the zucchini inedible. I know my discipline needs improving.

Maybe you're like Jennifer, who tried to ignore stress in order to maintain her sanity. Every bill she received in the mail went straight into the trash because, as she said, "It was just more bad news."

Zheng was a young college student who struggled to understand the US economic system. It stressed him out because he heard employers consider credit reports when hiring and he didn't have any credit.

John, a high school sophomore, helped his family pay rent. Despite not knowing how to budget, John wanted to spend time with friends, and had difficulty balancing school and life.

Maybe you can relate to Kevin and Julisa, who wanted to move into a stable home and neighborhood with their newborn baby. The bank denied their loan because their debt-to-income ratio was too high. Kevin was freelancing and unable to show enough steady income for the mortgage. It devastated them.

Katie was a single mom, stressed over how to give her son the best life possible. Every time she tried to save money, she turned around to find that Travis had grown out of his clothes. There was always something to buy. More food. Sports fees and uniforms. New hobbies. The expenses seemed endless. It felt impossible to save.

Alicia was a master's degree graduate working in a homeless shelter. Student loan debt, a low social services wage, and the high cost of living burdened her. She shared about the emotional roller coaster of entering a career to help people while being a paycheck away from needing the same help she provided.

For military service members, a negative credit history can be career-ending. I've seen financial worries terrify teenage recruits and also Stephen, a high-ranking officer, who needed help to manage his debt and household expenses.

The government considers financial capability essential to national security. According to National Security Guidelines, "Failure to live within one's means, satisfy debts, and meet financial obligations may indicate poor self-control, lack of judgment, or unwillingness to abide by rules and regulations, all of which can raise questions about an individual's reliability, trustworthiness, and ability to protect classified or sensitive information."[3]

The ability to manage money helps people function in society, survive in a world of challenges, and even build dream lives. Here is an unfortunate truth: personal abilities do not always determine outcomes.

The gap between the rich and poor has increased significantly over the last few decades. The Statista Research Department reported in 2023 that 68% of the total wealth in the United States was owned by the top 10 percent of earners. In comparison, the lowest 50% of earners combined owned only 3.3% of the total wealth.[4] Many strive to build wealth, but income inequality makes it difficult.

While knowledge alone won't eliminate disparities, the facts and examples in this book can improve understanding about economic history and the world of personal finance. By utilizing the "each one teach one" practice we can improve our finances, share information to help loved ones, and build powerful, thriving communities.

I've had the pleasure of helping the people in the examples above, and many more. I've wiped their tears and calmed their anxieties. We worked together, we found solutions, and they reached seemingly impossible goals. I can help you too. Guaranteed. That's why I wrote this book.

Stress affects all of us. It's not confined to a race, background, or socioeconomic status. We all want financial security. We work hard. But when stress becomes overwhelming, our situation can seem hopeless. Sometimes we all need help to determine the next best step toward a more hopeful life.

Stick with me, and I'll show you how you can reduce money-related stress and reach financial goals you never thought were possible.

I can help you learn:

- How values, mindset, and behaviors affect your finances
- How to develop a budget that works for you
- How to grow your savings
- How to avoid predatory loans, scams, fraud, and identity theft
- Strategies for building wealth and living a rich life
- Practical tips to help you manage debt and improve your credit score

This book is filled with the collective knowledge and wisdom from my own life and from the many people who taught me—mentors and clients alike. The wisdom written on these pages is from decades of teaching hundreds of workshops and coaching, counseling, and educating over 100,000 wonderful people.

The Latin phrase *Docendo discimus* applies to personal finance. It translates to "we learn from teaching."

I've had the benefit and joy of speaking with people from all stages in life. I'm always fascinated by the curious minds of young children and the humility of the elderly. My expertise isn't because of personal brilliance. My understanding of the financial world has come to life through listening to the knowledge, wisdom, and experiences of others.

Becoming financially capable is an ever-evolving journey. As Michelle Obama herself said in her bestselling memoir *Becoming*, "I see it instead as forward motion, a means of evolving, a way to reach continuously toward a better self. The journey doesn't end."[5]

Thank you for joining me on this learning adventure.

# PART I

## FINANCIAL ENVIRONMENT

Understanding Access and
Opportunity in a Turbulent World

# 1

# THE FINANCIAL WORLD WE LIVE IN

"Life's sloppy . . . You think you know how tomorrow's going
to be, you've made your plans, everything is set in place, and
then the unimaginable happens. Life catches you by surprise.
It always does. But there's good mixed in with the bad. It's
there. You just have to recognize it."[6]

—SUSAN BETH PFEFFER, FROM *THIS WORLD WE LIVE IN*

We can define financial environment in the broad sense
as many things. People often think about the economy,
about businesses, investors, and markets. You might think about
making money, gaining property, or growing wealth. I believe
the world is dynamic. It includes these items and more.

This world is not perfect. It's sloppy, messy, and at times
even broken. Greed, crime, and fraud are realities we live with.
Life is also full of beauty and wonder, which at times takes our
breath away. We cherish the loving kindness of family, the generosity from a stranger, or the comfort only a beloved pet can
provide. I'm not an economist. In fact, math as a subject doesn't
excite me, and I'm grateful for calculators. Though I've dabbled
in complex algorithms, my wife, a real scientist, and I joke about
the fact that I teach personal finance and discuss math; whereas
she actually uses math. She's the smart one in our house.

Some students ask me, "Why doesn't your wife teach the
class?" Well, the simple answer is that she's an introvert and not

a fan of the spotlight. Money is also about so much more than math. We can all agree that 1 plus 1 equals 2. That's easy. However, if we ask five people, "What's the best thing to do with two dollars?" we'll get at least six different opinions.

While teaching classes and workshops, I work hard to answer the WIIFM, "What's in it for me" question every student has. Some students, often the younger ones and teens, ask, "Yeah, but what's that got to do with me?" I appreciate the candor of youth who seek truth with amazing curiosity. With learning about personal finance, we all want to know how various principles apply on a personal level.

## Remain Curious and Question History

Diverse thinking can reduce bias, increase our worldview, and help us grow. Diverse thought allows us to imagine what could be. In the 1920s, the inventor Garrett Morgan saw a horrible accident and then thought, "How can driving be safer?" His curiosity led to the invention of traffic lights.[7]

George Washington Carver didn't accept the idea that his future was determined by history. He was born into slavery during the 1860s and overcame huge odds. He went to college and earned degrees in agricultural science. One of the many ways he made the world better was by teaching poor farmers how to improve their farming techniques.[8]

What do these examples have to do with me, you, or personal finance? Good question. To attain new goals, we must think and behave differently. Throughout life, we have a choice: accept things as they are, or embrace change. We can be like the impoverished farmers who refused Carver's new methods, or we can stay curious and grow beyond our wildest dreams.

When knowledge comes through family and friends, we often accept it as fact. Some tradition-based decisions, like how to celebrate holidays, bring joy and connect us to our familial roots.

Sometimes, we pass practices from one generation to the next without thinking.

The story goes like this: One day while a father was preparing a pot roast, his daughter asked about the recipe. He lovingly recalled the way his mother taught him how to cook the family favorite.

After watching him, she asked, "Dad, why do you cut the ends off the roast?"

"Well," said the father, "that's how my mom taught me."

The next time the young woman saw her grandmother, she asked, "Nana, why did you cut the ends off the roast before putting it into the oven to cook?"

"Well, sweetie, that's how my mother taught me the recipe and I always followed her instructions." She leaned in and whispered, "Let me tell you a secret." She continued loud enough that everyone in the room could hear. "One day, before your great-grandmother passed away, she shared all of her cooking techniques. The family was fortunate enough to have a gas stove then, a luxury that eliminated the need to labor over a hot wood fire. She explained how they always cut off the ends of the roast because their stove was small and the roasting pan that they owned was small. We cut the meat to fit the pan."

The three generations looked at each other and began laughing uncontrollably. They simultaneously realized how truly silly it was to perpetuate the tradition of cutting ends off a roast just because "that's what I learned."

## Be Informed

Many of us make small choices and life decisions based on traditions rather than on facts. We all have conscious or unconscious forces that nudge us to show favoritism toward or away from something or someone. These nudges are called biases and can be positive or negative. The book *Nudge* by Richard H. Thaler and Cass R. Sunstein is an excellent read.[9]

To make the best decisions for our health—our physical, social, emotional, spiritual, and, yes, even financial health—we need knowledge and wisdom. Making decisions rooted in myth, misinformation, or outdated information, like cutting off the ends of a large roast to fit into an oven, will lead to poor choices.

For example, "Don't put your money in a bank; they're crooks who steal hard-earned money."

"Debit cards will help you build credit."

"Never . . ." or "Always . . ."

"Carry a credit card balance to improve your credit score" is another misleading piece of advice. We'll discuss credit card utilization in a later chapter, but the only thing you'll gain by carrying a balance on revolving debt is more interest charges.

Some misinformation is intentional and predatory. Watch out for high-cost/high-risk alternative lenders who provide products like payday loans. These types of loans are where a borrower gets money and promises to pay it back with the next paycheck. Payday loans are very high cost, short-term loans that often leave borrowers in a vicious cycle of debt.

Be wary of companies that advertise, "Buy here, pay here—no credit, no problem." Many states have banned or limited crazy interest rates, while others like Idaho and Nevada still do not have any restrictions on finance charges.

To remain safe from wolves in sheep's clothing, we must become comfortable with financial products and services, understand their terms and cost, and learn how to use them to our advantage.

Much like in the story of the pot roast, many people watch how others use, or misuse, financial services and model them. I've had many friends and clients with healthy six-figure incomes who considered large debt payments a necessary part of life. The more money they made, the more they worked to keep up appearances of wealth.

The irony is that their lifestyle prevented them from accumulating assets, and in fact they were making the businesses rich from all the fees. I'm a fan of the proverb that suggests it is better to look poor and be rich than it is to look rich and be poor.

This can be difficult with persuasive marketing and a culture of consumer debt. While the world is sometimes sloppy, there is plenty of good to be found. To make wise consumer choices, we must do our research. The well-known broadcaster Walter Cronkite said, "Whatever the cost of our libraries, the price is cheap compared to that of an ignorant nation."[10]

# MONEY TALK Q&A

## Q: Where can I learn more about financial history?

A: Understanding history helps us make sense of the messy world we live in. Some influential resources include:

- *Why Nations Fail: The Origins of Power, Prosperity, and Poverty* by James A. Robinson

- *Global Economic History: A Very Short Introduction* by Robert C. Allen

- The Museum of American Finance (https://www.moaf.org/)

- FRED is an online database short for Federal Reserve Economic Data (https://fred.stlouisfed.org/)

- Foundation for Economic Education (https://fee.org/)

> Bonus: For resources about predatory lending, how to access trusted financial products and services, and more, check out the free bonuses at www.MattParadise.com/capablebonus.

# 2

# THE REALITY ABOUT MONEY

## We Hate (and Love) to Talk about It

Money is too often a taboo topic. Many people don't like to discuss it and leave managing it to the "professionals." I've counseled several people who ignored their debt statements out of fear. They told me that their bills contained bad news and just threw them in the trash.

Writers from various publications have reported on the topic of money taboos. Google it. The *New York Times, US News & World Report, Forbes*, and many other publications have published about the topic. I visited one of my favorite places recently, a public library. This library is in an exclusive suburb of Boston called Brookline. In the restroom hangs a sign to help patrons identify "Sensitive Subjects." The sign reads, "We're always here to help, but sometimes it's hard to ask." Topics include abortion, drug addiction, rape, race issues, and finances.[11]

The library serves and reflects the sentiments of the surrounding community. Finances are a difficult topic for conversation. Few want to be labeled an idiot by asking questions they feel everyone should know. We don't need to get into it further here, other than to state: many people are reluctant to discuss financial topics. Yes, even to the point of calling the reluctance a taboo.

Maybe you've experienced reluctance when speaking about money. Maybe you've seen others clumsily dance around the topic. I get it. It's difficult to talk about money. It's personal. Employees have been fired for trying to compare salaries or wages. Financial stress has led to divorce. Poor financial decisions are enveloped with shame. We don't want to be the one to ask questions about topics that "everyone should know."

Emotions around money are complicated. I've heard more than one person say, "I have too many bills and not enough cash to pay them, so screw it, I'm going shopping."

Here's the thing: keeping money a taboo topic keeps us poor. Problems don't go away when we ignore them. Let's talk about money. I guarantee that even the most challenging problems have a solution.

## Know the Cost

Another hot topic that borders on taboo is how much we pay for stuff. Airlines and hotels are notorious for the practice of charging different rates for the same seats or rooms and would prefer that you not discuss the price you paid. Car dealers thrive on a "hidden fee" business model. Fees within the financial sector are also shrouded in secrecy.

Do you have investments or retirement accounts? Do you understand their costs? Be sure of this: fees affect wealth building. During the COVID-19 pandemic, lawsuits about 401(k) expenses flooded courts. A Bloomberg Law analysis found that there was a fivefold increase in class action lawsuits challenging plan fees between 2019 and 2020.[12]

Several years ago, I helped a group of employees with a horrible retirement plan. The plan had very few options to invest in, they underperformed, and they had some of the highest fees ever. As a specific example, one of the limited options available was a bond that was primarily "invested" in cash. As you might imagine, cash will not produce high returns because, accounting for inflation, your "invested" money will lose value. This fund had an expense ratio—meaning the charges for handling money—higher than the target return. I mean, come on! If you put your money in this fund, it guaranteed you to lose money.

When the person responsible for administering the retirement plan was confronted, she said that it would require too much work to change the plan. Too much paperwork.

The Employee Retirement Income Security Act of 1974 (ERISA) is a federal law that sets minimum standards for most voluntarily established retirement and health plans in private industry to protect participating individuals.[13] "Too much paperwork" or "I just don't understand" does not excuse employers from their legal responsibilities.

Okay, my tirade is over. Thanks for hanging in there with me.

A difference of 1% or 2% may not sound like a lot, but consider this: NerdWallet authors analyzed a variety of scenarios and found that paying just 1% in fees could cost a young adult more than $590,000 in sacrificed returns over forty years of saving.[14]

Sixty-one percent of Americans don't know how much they pay for their investments, according to Personal Capital, an online adviser. About one-third of people also believe (falsely) that higher fees for investments translate to higher returns.[15] Remember that pot roast?

Let's get back to your question, "What's in it for me?" Or even better, "What's that got to do with me?" In a word: lots.

17

When talking about money is taboo, the flow of information rarely works in the best interests of consumers—that's you and me. Some people who work in the financial services industry are really salespeople. Their title may be educator, adviser, or something professional-sounding, but their job is to sell. It is business after all.

Don't get me wrong; skilled advisers, educators, and institutions that truly work for the best interests of their clients are plentiful. It is possible to serve people over profit. Many businesses discover that serving people with fairness and dignity can lead to greater profit. It is important for us to be educated. Just like you know better than to pay $100 for a gallon of milk or $1,000 for a carrot, do not overpay for financial products and services.

The reality of the world in which we live is that many in the top 1% built wealth from the excessive expenses paid by many of the rest of us. The wealthy understand the power of compound interest and asset appreciation, and they use wealth-building tools to their benefit.

## We Don't Talk About ...

Another reality of our world shrouded in mystery, myth, and misunderstanding is credit and debt.

I've sat behind tables at educational fairs and observed grown adults literally turn and walk away (quickly) when they hear "credit counseling." I've helped clients recover from shame and guilt while they wrestled with a low credit score. For some, a credit score is more than math; it's a symbol of success and reputation.

While I don't agree with that sentiment, there are many emotions with finances. In some of the homeless shelters where

I had the privilege of serving, shelter directors and staff had a hard time talking about credit and debt with clients. One significant reason was that they themselves also carried debt and, with it, many emotions, including embarrassment.

And please don't buy into the stereotypes that poor people are poor because of their own bad choices. There are many reasons someone might need to live in a homeless shelter. Some are fleeing from domestic violence, others suffer discrimination, while others are dealing with the aftermath of a sudden and unexpected illness or a physical disability. Poverty is a taboo subject, but a reality for households across the country.

While some claim that all debt is bad, others get rich using OPM (other people's money). A loan on a property that appreciates in value or produces positive cash flow is a powerful wealth generator. On the flip side, if someone gets a mortgage to occupy a home beyond their means, economic ruin could be right around the corner. When using debt to create additional assets, such as property or even a college degree, it *can* be good.

Student debt is *sometimes* a brilliant investment. Many lucrative careers in fields such as science, finance, and medicine begin with the help of student loans. It's important to consider careers and earnings, lifestyle, cost, and return on investment (ROI).

As of September 2022, the total outstanding federal and private US student loan debt was $1.76 trillion.[16] If you don't owe some of that money, I guarantee someone close to you does. Here's a simple college ROI calculator from the Federal Reserve Bank: https://www.frbsf.org/education/teacher-resources/value-of-college/.

I'll cover credit in greater detail later in this book, but, for now, remember that employers, landlords, and loan officers consider it when making critical decisions that affect you. Not all debt is bad, and harnessing the power of OPM can be magnificent.

## Learn the Facts and Talk about Money

My encouragement is simple: Have conversations about money and never stop learning. Speak with your significant other, family, and friends. Discuss money matters with children. And plan. One of my mentors, Leo MacNeil, often said, "If you don't have a plan for your money, someone else does."

Some financial "professionals" gain just enough knowledge to sell their products and services. They are happy to give advice for a price. Equally dangerous are consumers who ignore trustworthy help. Both groups of people learn just enough to gain confidence in their own abilities, but fail at delivering wealth building strategies. Neither scenario is good.

Fear and taboo often go hand in hand. It's easy to be swayed by fear, and many predators use fear to advance their cause like terrorism, isolationism, and other -isms. *Psychology Today* provides a warning and simple advice to those with depressive tendencies: stay away from traditional fear-based media. Psychologists explain that news programming uses a hierarchy, "if it bleeds, it leads," and consuming this kind of programming may be detrimental to our health.[17]

I learned about worldwide poverty and starvation through fear-based tactics. Maybe you heard a similar speech: "Finish everything on your plate; there are starving children who would be happy to have something to eat!"

I find it overwhelming to listen to, watch, or read traditional news. Here are some stress-causing headlines written in 2022:

- "Cryptocurrencies Melt Down in a 'Perfect Storm' of Fear and Panic," from the *New York Times*.[18]
- CNN published, "More than $7 trillion has been wiped out from the stock market this year."[19]

Fearmongering for profit isn't new. In 1929, newspapers had a field day publishing stories of stockbrokers throwing themselves out of windows to their demise. The media painted a grim picture and communicated to their readership, "If you lose money, life isn't worth living." The reality was much different. According to John Kenneth Galbraith in his book, *The Great Crash 1929*, there was not a correlation between the stock market crash and suicidal investors or brokers.[20]

Our goal isn't to determine which economic half-truth is least harmful. As Ben Franklin said, "Half a truth is often a great lie."[21] Our goal as consumers is to determine the facts and make the best possible choices based on the information.

# MONEY TALK Q&A

**Q:** What are some good questions to get my family or friends talking about personal finance and economics?

**A:** Conversations with friends and loved ones about money are really important. Consider their thoughts and opinions as you work toward unity. Ask yourselves: How are you feeling about our finances? What are your dreams and goals? What can we do to reach our goals? What are we doing well? What do you think we need to change?

There isn't an age that's too young to introduce financial concepts. Double-check to see that content is developmentally and culturally appropriate. There are lots of financial education resources for kids and adults. You can find hundreds of examples by searching the Jump$tart Clearinghouse (https://jumpstartclearinghouse.org/).

Bonus: Check out the free resources at
www.MattParadise.com/capablebonus
for financial education content and worksheets to
start conversations and break money taboos.

# 3

# IS MONEY THE ROOT OF ALL EVIL?

Few other topics generate as much discussion as money. It's more than math. Think about it. How many people get emotional about 1 + 1? However, when you add dollar signs to the conversation, all types of opinions surface.

Letting emotions control us can be dangerous. As the poet Oscar Wilde said, "I don't want to be at the mercy of my emotions. I want to use them, to enjoy them, and to dominate them."[22]

Fortunately, we can master our emotions. There are, however, parts of wealth building beyond our control. Corporate layoffs leave households jobless. Rising costs impact personal budgets. Unexpected health challenges cause financial problems. High interest rates make homeownership difficult.

It's helpful to understand influences beyond our day-to-day control. To better understand broader financial conditions, I'll break down an economic system into six parts: central banks, regulatory agencies, institutions, markets, financial instruments, and money. Let's discuss each.

## Central Banks (the Bank for Banks)

Central banks are known as *reserve banks* or a monetary authority. They are different from local institutions, since they manage currencies, the money supply, and interest rates. Central banks also provide stability to member institutions by lending to the banking sector and providing supervisory and regulatory powers.

You may have heard of Federal Reserve banks. They are much less a bank and more of a system with twelve regional banks and a board. In the United States, on December 23, 1913, Congress passed the Federal Reserve Act, which created our system of central banking. After multiple economic panics, people wanted central control of the monetary system in order to ease future financial crises.

The Federal Reserve System, "the Fed," helps to stabilize the US economic system and promote consumer protection and community development. One way the central bank helps bring stability is through its influence on inflation. The Fed intervenes in currency, debt, and equity markets to maintain the targeted rate of inflation considered healthy for our economy, which is about 2% annually.

In 2022, the inflation rate in the US rose above 9% for the first time in decades. When the rate of inflation gets too high, the Fed raises interest rates to slow the economy and prevent the out-of-control inflation.

Managing inflation is part of economic prosperity. During the COVID-19 pandemic, direct government stimulus checks and low interest rates combined to entice consumers to buy more stuff. These factors increased demand so much that we experienced supply shortages and huge price spikes. Lumber or toilet paper anyone?

I've worked with the Fed and have seen how the organization strengthens communities. Policy decisions aside, programs like the Working Cities Challenge, financial education, and direct help to reduce income disparities have stabilized vulnerable populations throughout the country.[23]

## Regulatory Agencies (Government Involvement)

You may or may not agree with the government getting involved with regulation and oversight, but consumers need protection.

Some groups are probably familiar to you. If you've ever been in a bank or credit union, there's a good chance that you've leaned against a small sign with the letters FDIC or NCUA. The signs are tiny and easy to miss, and free lollipops are distracting. The Federal Deposit Insurance Corporation (FDIC) and the National Credit Union Administration (NCUA), among other duties, provide deposit insurance to depositors.

Some agencies supervise and assist with specific sections of the economy, such as the FDIC and NCUA. There are many more letter combinations in the alphabet soup of government agencies that provide specific public services.

This section is boring for some, and you might wonder, "What's in it for me?" Deposit insurance means that if a financial institution goes out of business—it happens more often than you might think—your money is still safe. Even if an insured bank or credit union gets robbed or burns down, you will not lose your money. No depositor has ever lost a penny of insured deposits since President Franklin D. Roosevelt created the FDIC in 1933.[24]

These federal agencies do a bunch of other stuff besides providing insurance. They get involved in consumer protection, education, and industry analysis, to name a few. I've worked with both organizations and have found them to have helpful resources. You can see what they offer and how they might help on their respective websites: www.fdic.gov and www.ncua.gov. The people who work there are passionate about helping others.

For example, when I started in financial education over twenty years ago, Paul Horwitz with the FDIC Alliance for Economic Inclusion was one of the first people I met. He mentored with great patience, wit, and wisdom. I had the pleasure of working with him on several projects, and it was always a learning experience.

His mentorship allowed me to identify shady businesses, help people steer clear of them, and choose safe wealth building tools. Regulations ensure everybody can access safe and affordable financial products and services.

## Financial Institutions (Think: Banks and Credit Unions)

Those who handle transactions between people saving money and people spending money are called financial institutions. The US Treasury's definition includes someone doing business in places like money services companies, casinos, or a person subject to supervision by any state or federal bank authority.[25]

Two common types of financial institutions are banks and credit unions. They offer deposit accounts, loans, investments, insurance policies, and foreign currency exchange. Both have many of the same products and services, but banks are for-profit institutions while credit unions are not-for-profit and distribute their profits among their members.

Credit unions will probably offer you lower-cost services and better interest rate options for both loans and deposits. Large banks may offer more services, products, and advanced technology. Local community banks and credit unions offer more free accounts, charge fewer fees, provide personalized attention, and reinvest local dollars back into the community.

Financial institutions have an important role in the economy. Some consumers who lack access to mainstream banking turn to expensive "check cashers" on payday. These businesses charge a percentage between 1% and 12%, *just to cash a check*.

When choosing the best institution and account, it's important we first consider our unique needs, understand the cost, and shop around to find the best fit.

## Financial Markets (Like a Grocery Store for Investments)

Food is a big deal. Most of us don't have the land, skills, or resources to provide everything we need to eat. We rely on those who can. Grocery stores are necessary because they provide the convenience of bringing food to one place in the community. The stores don't grow the food themselves; they provide the opportunity for shoppers to buy and growers/manufacturers to sell in one place.

Financial markets are similar. On my own, I don't have the talents, time, and resources to run multiple corporations. Businesses need cash to operate. They get the money by selling stocks and bonds through a financial market. The market can be a physical location, like the New York Stock Exchange (NYSE), or online, like the National Association of Securities Dealers Automated Quotations (you may have heard it called NASDAQ).

Each time that someone buys or sells a financial instrument, the transaction is called a trade. In the United States alone, there are billions of trades in a day.[26]

## Financial Instruments (Stocks, Bonds, and More)

A financial instrument[27] is the contract for assets and liabilities with any kind of monetary value. There are two sides to the contract. One side has the item of value, known as the asset. The other side has debt, which is called a liability. Think of it like this: assets put money in your pocket, while liabilities take money out.

When you put money, *deposit*, into a savings account you're using a financial instrument. The financial institution owes you money and will pay you *interest* to keep it safe. The bank or credit union makes money by providing loans to borrowers at a higher interest rate.

Stocks and bonds are common examples of financial instruments. Owning stock, also called a *share*, means partial ownership of a company. Yes, it's possible to be a co-owner of your favorite business. Bonds are loans and act like an IOU. They can be from a business or even from a government.

Other instruments are more complex, like credit default swaps, derivatives, and bespoke tranche opportunities. Many complicated products are not only difficult to understand, they can be risky for investors and the entire economy.

Don't stress if these terms and concepts are new. Your curiosity, positive mindset, and action will reap dividends. We'll cover investing later in this book.

## Money (Do I need to say more?)

Smackers, c-notes, dead presidents, Benjamins, bucks, bones, clams, dough, moolah, bread, guap—money has many aliases. Economists with the media outlet *Shmoop* define money as something that serves as a medium of exchange, a unit of accounting, and a store of value.[28] Whatever we call it, our financial system functions because we all agree to accept money when making transactions.

## Is it Evil?

You've likely heard the phrase, "Money is the root of all evil." It incorrectly came from the Bible. The actual phrase is "For the love of money is a root of all kinds of evil."[29] When we love money more than anything else, it will lead to trouble. It's harmful when businesses put profit before people. Capitalism, for the sake of itself, creates cannibalism. Money alone is not evil; it's a soulless, non-living thing. How it's used makes all the difference.

# MONEY TALK

**Q: Where can I learn more about economics and financial principles?**

A: Ray Dalio, a successful investor and entrepreneur, wrote the bestselling book *Principles.* He has many helpful (and free) videos (https://www.youtube.com/@principlesbyraydalio/videos).

Check out *How The Economic Machine Works* by Ray Dalio: https://www.youtube.com/watch?v=PHe0bXAIuk0.

The Foundation for Economic Education (FEE) (https://fee .org/) is also a great resource. It's a nonprofit educational foundation and provides free online courses, in-person seminars, free books for classrooms, and daily online content.

Bonus: You can find helpful information about our
financial system, financial institutions,
and the products and services they offer here:
www.MattParadise.com/capablebonus.

# 4

# I'M NOT A *HOMO ECONOMICUS*

## Economics and Irrational Behavior

Studying the economy is no joke. Seriously, I Googled economics jokes for this chapter and didn't laugh at a single one.

Economics is a serious topic. It considers how the economy works. Economics combines politics, sociology, psychology, business, and history. It examines human behavior, decisions, and reactions.

Macroeconomics is the study of the big picture of the economy, such as inflation, price levels, rate of economic growth, national income, balance of payment equilibrium, income equality, gross domestic product (GDP), and changes in unemployment. These collective areas measure how the overall economy is doing.[30]

Microeconomics considers the small stuff: people and companies and the effects of their individual decisions. Topics include supply and demand, scarcity (the concept that we might have unlimited wants, but limited means or resources), and competitive advantage.[31]

Besides macro- and microeconomics, there is behavioral economics. This study combines psychology and economics to understand how and why people behave the way they do.

None of these disciplines exists on its own. The "big picture stuff" affects our day-to-day decisions and vice versa. Because this book focuses on personal finance and not economics, this chapter is brief, but it's helpful to understand economic context as we make personal decisions.

## More Than Money

When most people think about economics, they associate it with money. The field of study encompasses much more than money; it's about making choices. Economics includes decisions about everything from who we vote for to how we spend our time and why we set certain personal goals.

Macroeconomics is the study of forces that affect an entire economy. We'll get into the "small stuff" and individual decisions later in the book. Macroeconomics, as defined by the World Bank, "is the system that connects the countless policies, resources, and technologies that make economic development happen. Without proper macro management, poverty reduction and social equity are not possible."[32]

Macroeconomics includes the big picture stuff over which we have little control. The tricky thing about studying the subject is that economists don't agree on which factors affect an economy the most. Bill Gates, the Microsoft cofounder, said, "Too bad economists don't actually understand macroeconomics. It's not like physics where you take certain inputs and you predict certain outputs."[33]

Traditional economists have portrayed people within the economy as *homo economicus,* the dollar-searching man.[34] This is a play on words, combining *homo sapiens* and *economics.* The portrayal is almost robotic. Picture a person who consistently acts rationally, in their own self-interest, and who pursues goals and objectives in the most optimal way. I mean, come on, I've met no one like that. I've had spirited debates with at least one economist on the topic.

The idea that people always act rationally is preposterous. People are imperfect. As someone who has struggled with addiction, I know all too well that decisions can be self-destructive and far from rational. By grace, hard work, and the love of family and friends, I've been sober for over twenty years. It is still a challenge to ignore marketing pressures.

When a company develops a marketing and advertising plan, their goal is to separate consumers from their money. Successful strategies appeal to our emotions. They want us to feel like we *need* the product or service, and we'll become better people with the purchase.

The study of behavioral economics helps us understand why we choose what we choose. Our decisions can be so consistently counterintuitive that noted *New York Times* bestselling author and psychology and behavioral economics professor Dan Ariely wrote the book *Predictably Irrational.*[35] Dan skillfully explains how we fail to make smart, rational choices. "From drinking coffee to losing weight, from buying a car to choosing a romantic partner, we consistently overpay, underestimate, and procrastinate. Yet, these misguided behaviors are neither random nor senseless. They're systematic and predictable—making us predictably irrational." Hidden forces influence our decisions. The greater our understanding of psychology and behavior, the more productive we'll be in reaching our financial goals.

Did you know that retailers have spent many millions of dollars to understand and manipulate consumer behavior? For instance, when you need food staples like bread and milk, the items aren't conveniently located in the grocery store. They manipulate consumer behavior by intentionally placing items so that while consumers meander toward the back of the store, they pick up additional items. Have you ever shopped with a child who constantly grabbed items at checkout? Wouldn't it be easier if the lanes were clear of distraction? Well, at some point you've probably grabbed gum, a candy bar, or other high-margin item on impulse.

Our sense of smell is incredible. Scents can have powerful ties to emotions and memory. Researchers at Washington State University found that simple scents are powerful motivators for spending. Some retailers intentionally pump in certain aromas to trigger feelings associated with the brand. Real estate agents are taking advantage of this idea when they use candles or fresh-baked cookies to help sell properties. Who doesn't love the smell of a good cookie?

As humans, we're emotional and easily distracted. Businesses leverage this vulnerability for profit, and the use of behavioral economics has increased in recent years. Have you ever shopped online and noticed that if you didn't buy a certain item immediately, it would sell out? Have you ever found your online shopping much faster and easier than when you're in a store? Did you ever buy something you didn't need because of the "no risk trial" and kept it because keeping it was easier than returning it? I have.

Just the other day, I bought an online course because of the temporary discount. If I didn't buy it right away, the price would have doubled. They nudged me. Someone has nudged you, and you might not have noticed. The more we're aware of marketing and retail nudges, the more control we have over our decisions. Educated consumers are savvy consumers who make wise choices. Sometimes.

We can't control any of the "big picture stuff" like inflation, which lowers the purchasing power of money; or the Consumer Price Index (CPI), which measures the change in prices we pay for goods and services. While we don't have power over the crazy cost of food, we can control our reactions to the economy. Economics starts at home. My family eats less meat to lower the grocery bill. I try to avoid expensive and unhealthy snacks. The "best" decisions for my wallet and waistline are challenging to make. I am irrational, but I strive to make healthy choices. After all, health is wealth; but that's a topic for another chapter.

# MONEY TALK

Q: Where can I learn more about microeconomics and financial behavior?

A: The Decision Lab runs one of the largest publications in applied behavioral science. Their website has a great knowledge center: https://thedecisionlab.com/.

You can take free online microeconomics (and other) courses to build your skills and advance your career at https://www.edx.org/learn/microeconomics.

The film version of the bestselling book *Freakonomics: A Rogue Economist Explains the Hidden Side of Everything* by Steven Levitt and Stephen J. Dubner is available free on You-Tube: https://www.youtube.com/watch?v=IZ5GOpy0yzM.

Economics is an enormous field of study with outstanding books and resources to dig into. For free access to more information, check out www.MattParadise.com/capablebonus.

# 5

## DEFERRED DREAMS AND SKIN COLOR

### Prejudice Makes Us All Poorer

R acism within our economy is real. And it's complicated. And it's emotional. It affects everyone. The term *racism* represents different things to different people. For this book, we'll use the Australian Human Rights Commission definition:

> *Racism is the process by which systems and policies, actions and attitudes create inequitable opportunities and outcomes for people based on race. Racism is more than just prejudice in thought or action. It occurs when this prejudice—whether individual or institutional—is accompanied by the power to discriminate against, oppress or limit the rights of others.*[36]

With racism, we have a choice. We can ignore it and perpetuate the very thing that destroys families, neighborhoods, and communities, or we can confront the realities and work toward healing.

Adam Smith was a Scottish economist, moral philosopher, and author and considered the father of capitalism. You don't have to agree with his philosophy; however, his beliefs and writings have affected the economy and our lives. I agree with his quote: No society can surely be flourishing and happy, of which the far greater part of the members are poor and miserable.[37]

We can't escape the fact that our careers, our purchases, and our lives are intertwined. It's inescapable. We've seen this come into play during the global COVID-19 pandemic in disheartening and grievous ways.

The Boston Celtics introduced me to the concept of *ubuntu*. In 2002, Doc Rivers of the Boston Celtics adopted it as a rallying call—they even inscribed *ubuntu* on their championship rings in 2008. Don't worry if you're not a fan of the Celtics or basketball. The concept applies to everyone.

*Ubuntu* came from a Zulu phrase, which expresses that a person is a person through other people. It means, "I am, because you are."[38]

Our economic system works best when it works for everyone. Systemic barriers within the economy not only impoverish the minority, but also affect the entire economy.

## "Those People"

I haven't been the target of prejudice because of my skin color. I'm seen as a White man. It extended privilege to me based on those two genetic traits, even when I didn't know disparities existed. At the same time, I am the product of mixed races. My mother is pasty White. Red hair and freckles, the whole nine yards. Her parents were of English and French ancestry.

My father is mixed race. His mother was French, while his father was dark-skinned Jamaican. My dad is fair-skinned, but I've never seen him with a sunburn. In the sun, he gets darker and darker. His hair, when he had more of it, was black and very curly.

If you've seen my picture, you'll know whose genes are visible. Let's put it this way: I don't tan. In the sun I turn lobster-red, I peel, and then I turn pasty again. I also have a mixed-race marriage. I have never been a victim of racism. My wife, who is of Asian descent, has. She's been spat upon because she looks "different." The idea of racism is controversial and polarizing.

I've heard confusion about systemic versus individual racism. To help clarify: individual racism has to do with personal assumptions, beliefs, attitudes, and actions that reinforce racism. This type of racism may gain strength or stem from socioeconomic histories but occurs person-to-person or small-group level. Think of slurs, racial jokes, and statements like these:

- "It was just my opinion."
- "It didn't really cause harm to anyone."
- "I'm not racist, I just—"
- "I'm color blind; I just don't see race or color."
- "Not in my backyard (NIMBY)."
- "Those people."

There's a good chance you've heard a similar comment. Maybe you ignored it. Maybe you confronted it. If we're gut-level honest with ourselves, we may remember a time when we used a phrase and cast it off as politically incorrect. This is not about being PC. This is about families. It's about people and prejudices perpetuated. Abstinence from ignorant phrases alone heals no wounds. Education can, however, overcome ignorance.

Edna, a great friend and civil rights activist, told me, "If you're color blind, then you can't see me." As a ninety-year-old African American woman born and raised in Boston, she

39

has experienced discrimination throughout her life. If we just ignore those experiences and that reality, then we miss the point of social justice.

We must see, listen to, celebrate, and learn from each other's differences. Sometimes, too often, we may not even understand our own racial bias. I have one family member who insists that she's not racist and has said nothing racist. Yet she has made comments when driving through a mixed-race neighborhood such as "hold on to your wallet."

As I write this, we're in the middle (prayerfully, near the end) of the COVID-19 pandemic. Another family member said, "I will not eat Chinese food until this virus mess is over." Some Americans referred to the deadly coronavirus as "The Chinese Virus," which led to anti-Asian stigma and discrimination. Maybe you've heard friends, loved ones, or even strangers say something similar. It might seem harmless. Make no mistake, words are powerful and they have consequences.

Misinformation about the virus encouraged racist memes that portrayed Chinese people as bat eaters responsible for spreading the virus, and reviving century-old myths about Asian food being dirty. Racist jokes led to violence. According to the Center for the Study of Hate and Extremism, anti-Asian hate crime increased by 339 percent in 2021.[39]

Let's connect the dots and focus on the economy and personal finance. It's appropriate for you to ask, "What does racism have to do with me?"

The National Bureau of Economic Research (NBER) examined the financial effects of COVID-19. He found that, "Racial disparities in business formation raise concerns about lost economic efficiency. If minority entrepreneurs face liquidity constraints, discrimination, or other barriers to creating new businesses or expanding current ones, there will be efficiency losses in the economy."[40]

Economic efficiency is important because it allows businesses to reduce costs and increase production. In simple terms, the research found that racism makes the stuff we buy more expensive.

## Bigger Than One-to-One

Individual racism is a huge issue, but for this book, I'd like to focus a bit more on systemic racism[41], which is very much a part of the financial environment. Systemic racism excludes or promotes particular groups of people based on their cultural and racial identities. The racist practices are often deeply entrenched in institutions' policies and procedures.

Institutional racism[42] includes discrimination inserted in the laws and regulations of a society or an organization. It's too easy to oversimplify or misattribute wealth disparities by thinking that poverty is only because of a person's choices and behaviors. Maybe you've heard something like, "If a person or group only worked harder and saved more, then they would have more." This sentiment is one I've heard many times. In fact, my wife and I discussed race and wealth accumulation with a family member who said that people are poor because they make poor decisions and don't work hard enough.

The conversation became tense as the family member continued and said, "Some cultures are just lazy and not clean."

My wife and I called the comments what they were: racist. Stereotypes perpetuated by family members rather than experience or facts influenced the individual. The reasons for poverty are many. Some of the hardest working people I've met are poor. So, the question we might ask is why? Why do some ethnic groups have far less wealth? What explains the racial differences in resource transfers across generations?

The reasons are extensive and complicated. Some factors include racial disparities in education, race-based wage gaps, redlining, and other lending practices that have prevented Black, Indigenous, and People of Color from accumulating wealth. The disparities aren't behind us. Published research from multiple sources shows that the racial wealth divide has grown increasingly worse during the last fifty years.[43]

The racial wealth gap affects the entire economy. Racist policies have denied millions of people jobs, quality education, and access to financial products and services. This limits income, wealth building, and generational wealth transfer and perpetuates cycles of poverty. As mentioned earlier, this injustice makes the stuff we buy more expensive.

In 2020, Citigroup released a study titled "Closing the Racial Inequality Gaps: The Economic Cost of Black Inequality in the US."[44] Their research revealed that the economic impact of not addressing racial gaps between Blacks and Whites has cost the US economy $16 trillion over the past twenty years.

The International Monetary Fund (IMF) is an organization of 190 countries that works to secure sustainable economic growth and reduce poverty around the world. They project that the racial wealth gap will cost the US economy between $1 trillion and $1.5 trillion in lost consumption and investment during the ten-year span ending in 2028.[45]

In simple terms, racism is bad and has cost the economy lots of money. Without significant change, racism will cost all of us lots more money.

The purpose of learning history is not solely for pursuing education; rather, it can help avoid unnecessary mistakes in the future. If we don't eliminate racial disparities, the economic losses to our economy and each of us personally will continue to increase.

While the loss to the entire economy is significant, the losses for individual families are catastrophic. If you look at the data, you'll see the disparities are stark across the board, from savings rates to retirement accounts. The inequities are present in schools, jobs, homeownership, and wealth building. Consider the fact that, according to the US Census in 2022, for every dollar the median Non-Hispanic White American has, the median Black and Hispanic American has only about 10 cents.[46]

## Shut Out of Education and the Economy

Okay, so maybe you're wondering what this has to do with the overall financial environment and becoming financially capable. You might even question if this chapter applies to your life. Racism is part of our economic reality. Besides being reprehensible, it has a negative impact on our economy and society.

You understand that a higher income increases the opportunity to create wealth. It's challenging to build financial security with little to no money.

Systemic disparities have a significant impact on wealth, health, education, and the ability to earn money. The National Bureau of Economic Research examined why the Black unemployment rate has been twice that of Whites. The researchers found that job applicants with White-sounding names get called back about 50% more of the time than applicants with Black-sounding names, even when they have identical résumés.[47]

Education can change the trajectory of one's life. As a general rule, the more education someone has, the more money they earn over their lifetime. Education *can* be a powerful pathway out of poverty. Racial segregation in schools isn't an anecdote or a thing of the past. Racial minorities are often denied high-quality education.

It's been six decades since the case of *Brown v. Board of Education*[48] when the Supreme Court declared "separate but equal" unconstitutional. Our schools are just as much, if not more, segregated now than ever. Unaddressed school segregation is a major long-standing policy failure that relegates Black children to schools that put them behind. The educational gaps between White and Black children translate into difficulty earning a living wage and building wealth later in life.

According to the Economic Policy Institute, "Black children are more than twice as likely as white children to attend high-poverty schools."[49]

I've taught in high-poverty schools and have seen firsthand how demoralizing they can be. Because of overcrowding, there's not always a desk for each student in the classroom. There are outdated and tattered textbooks, and, even then, there's not always one available for each child. Imagine for a moment that you're a fifteen-year-old high school sophomore. You're inundated with social pressures, raging hormones, and all the awkwardness of puberty. You don't have a desk or a book to learn from. Would you feel supported in your education?

There are significant racial gaps in confronting students in college as well. A *Boston Globe* article was headlined "Debt load hits Black students hardest." The article noted that Black students on average owed 113% of their student loan twelve years later. Can you imagine paying your debts, only to have the balance increase? In contrast, White borrowers paid down their debt and owed only 65% of the original loan amount after twelve years.[50]

Multiple states' attorneys general filed lawsuits against student loan servicers for their predatory and "designed to fail" practices. In early 2022, Navient, a major student loan servicing company, settled allegations of abusive lending practices for $1.85 billion.[51]

For-profit colleges play a significant role in keeping ambitious men and women in poverty. As mentioned earlier, education can be life changing. According to the Brookings Institution, "For-profit colleges, more than any other type of institution, leave students taking on student debt while not having a degree to show for it."

The Brookings authors, Ariel Gelrud Shiro and Richard V. Reeves in the How We Rise series, continued, "Black and Latino students make up less than one-third of all college students, yet they represent nearly half of all who attend for-profit colleges. This results from predatory recruitment tactics targeted at Black and Latino communities."[52]

There have been hundreds of thousands of federal fraud complaints filed against for-profit colleges for lying about employment statistics and graduate incomes. In 2021, the Federal Trade Commission (FTC) announced that it would investigate 70 for-profit higher education institutions for the false promises about graduates' job prospects and expected earnings.

One year later, on February 16, 2022, the US Department of Education announced that 16,000 student borrowers would receive $415 million retribution.[53]

While the penalties were historic, they were a drop in the bucket relative to the damage caused to families over the last several decades. The burden of student debt combined with the lack of fair wage options has created a cycle of poverty that remains difficult to break.

Low wages keep homeownership out of reach for millions of people in the US. Since most states rely on local property taxes to fund public education, the areas with greater poverty have under-resourced schools.

In his decision in the landmark *Brown v. Board of Education* case, Chief Justice Earl Warren wrote:

"It is doubtful that any child may be expected to succeed in life if we deny the opportunity of an education. Such an opportunity, where the state has undertaken to provide it, is a right which must be made available to all on equal terms."[54]

It has been several decades since the landmark Supreme Court case, and education and homeownership, which provides the funds for quality learning, still aren't "available to all on equal terms."

## Locked Out of Housing

Safe and affordable housing can provide a solid foundation for households. Housing affects everything from improved economic stability to increased access to education.

Many Americans view owning a home as a primary means to accumulate wealth. Unfortunately, low-income households and households of color have limited access to homeownership. The limited supply of affordable housing, restricted access to credit, and systemic inequities create an economic burden that we bear as a nation.

Homeownership contributes significantly to individual wealth in America, and racial disparities in homeownership therefore affect how wealth is distributed across demographic groups. In 2019, the homeownership rate among White non-Hispanic Americans was 73.3%, compared to only 42.1% among Black Americans. This was the largest gap since the Census time series began. The data also show that Whites had a much higher return on investment.[55]

To help understand the lack of homeownership equity, we'll use a few historical facts from author and academic researcher Richard Rothstein. Among many credentials, he wrote *The Color of Law: A Forgotten History of How Our Government Segregated America.*

Working-class, immigrant, Black and White families lived in integrated neighborhoods during the early 1900s. However, in 1933, the federal government began a program called the New Deal that intentionally segregated America's housing. The New Deal was a series of programs, public work projects, financial reforms, and regulations enacted by President Franklin D. Roosevelt. The housing programs begun under the New Deal were equal to a "state-sponsored system of segregation," according to Rothstein.[56]

In his book, he outlines how the Federal Housing Administration (FHA), which was established in 1934, expanded the segregation efforts by refusing to insure mortgages in and near African-American neighborhoods. We know this racist policy as "redlining." The FHA also subsidized builders who were mass-producing entire subdivisions for whites and prohibited African-Americans.

Redlining discriminates against neighborhoods with low-income residents and significant numbers of racial and ethnic minorities by withholding investment.

Neighborhoods with a high proportion of minority residents are more likely to be redlined than other neighborhoods with similar household incomes, housing age and type, and other determinants of risk but different racial composition. The best-known examples of redlining include denied access to financial services like banking and insurance, credit rationing, as well as reduced access to healthcare, education, and even healthy food.[57]

The Fair Housing Act of 1968 outlawed the practice of redlining. However, the racist practices still exist.

The US Department of Housing and Urban Development (HUD) published a study called "Continued Discrimination Against People of Color." The study examined twenty-eight metropolitan areas and thousands of people. For data comparison, it paired two individuals based on gender and age. These people were well qualified to rent or buy an advertised unit. The only substantial difference in the pair was their race. One couple was White, and the other was Black, Latino, or Asian. The non-White home buyers were told about and shown fewer houses than White home buyers. They showed Asians almost 20% fewer housing units.[58]

Housing discrimination still impoverishes people today. On January 12, 2023, the Justice Department secured the largest redlining settlement agreement in history. The Attorney General secured over $75 million for Neighborhoods of Color. The initiative helps ensure that Black Americans and all Communities of Color can access the credit needed to purchase a home.[59]

Financial capability is about so much more than being educated and building wise practices and behaviors. Many factors beyond a family or an individual contribute to or impede success. To be financially capable as a nation, everyone needs equitable access and opportunity to build wealth.

We can learn from history and avoid the mistakes of the past. I need to remember that my life is intertwined with others—even when they may look or think differently than I do.

The horrors of our recent past affect today's generations. Without healing, racial tensions will continue. I hope this book will improve our understanding of inequities and help us strive toward justice for all and a *"more perfect union."*[60] I believe, and data support the fact, that what affects one of us affects all of us. Injustice is part of the world, but we can overcome it.

# MONEY TALK Q&A

**Q: Why are we still talking about race? Aren't we past this? Can't we just move on?**

A: No.

**Q: Doesn't "economic fairness" mean that those who have more need to sacrifice for those who have less?**

A: No. This might be true in game theory, but it's not how life works. Game theory and economic theory describe a zero-sum game as a situation where one side's gain is balanced by a corresponding loss on the other side. Investing in all communities (education, jobs, healthcare, housing, etc.) increases the collective human capital and economic opportunities.

For more on how health inequality affects quality of life, the economy, and national security, check out https://www .americanprogress.org/article/top-10-ways-to-improve-health -and-health-equity/.

Enhancing Equity to Improve Community Resilience (https:// icma.org/articles/pm-magazine/enhancing-equity-improve -community-resilience) is a well researched piece that links to sources like a study by Citi that shows that the nation's GDP would grow by $5 trillion by eliminating racial disparities.

The Federal Reserve Bank of San Francisco compiled essays to help with community development, "Investing in What Works for America's Communities" (https://www.frbsf.org/wp-content/uploads/sites/3/investing-in-what-works.pdf).

There is no shortage of research and data that show equitability is good for everyone. If you're interested in learning more about racial inequalities in our financial systems, check out these sites:

- Federal Reserve Bank St. Louis Institute for Economic Equity (www.stlouisfed.org/institute-for-economic -equity)
- RAND, Social and Economic Well-being Center (www.rand.org/well-being/racial-equity-policy.html)
- Economic Policy Institute (www.epi.org)

## Q: How do we fix racial and gender inequalities?

A: There is no simple answer to this trillion-dollar question. The data show disparities exist and they're bad for everyone.

Have racist systems improved with civil rights? Yes, however, the wealth and income gaps are still growing. It's terrible for local and national politics when 1 in 16 Black Americans cannot vote because of disenfranchisement laws. It's shameful and tragic that the mortality rate among Black infants in the US is more than twice that of White infants. The disparity is even worse in some urban areas.

Do women have greater agency since women's suffrage? Yes, but, over 100 years later, White women only make 82 cents for every dollar earned by men. The pay disparity is worse for Black, Indigenous, and Women of Color. This inequality is unjust for the over 72 million working women in the US.

Policy changes alone will not create systemic change. Racial and gender equitability also requires a social and cultural shift. Political strategies have merit; however, they are often limited by partisanship and election cycles. Even the best public programs will not create widespread change in a toxic environment. So back to the question: "How do we fix disparities?"

First, the answer starts with an acknowledgment that there are problems with our current financial systems. Not acknowledgment by a few people, but universal acceptance that racial and gender disparities exist and that eliminating these disparities is for the good of everyone.

Second, systemic problems call for systemic solutions. Great ideas exist to eliminate disparities in the criminal justice system; there's fantastic brainstorming to eliminate disparities in health care; and there are also great ideas to eliminate the racial wealth gap. Compartmentalized solutions fall short. Building whole health wealth depends on a universal approach. Health affects wealth and vice versa. Education is connected to earning capacity.

Third, change begins at home. Racism, sexism, and other discriminatory beliefs and behaviors are driven by stereotypes, fear, and ignorance. While I don't have the power to change the world, I can love my family. I can love my neighbor. Love has the power to drive out darkness, eliminate fear, and change the world.

Consider this your invitation to join me.

As Eleanor Roosevelt said, "Where, after all, do universal human rights begin? In small places, close to home—so close and so small that we cannot see them on any maps of the world. Yet they are the world of the individual person; the neighborhood he lives in; the school or college he attends; the factory, farm or office where he works. Such are the places where every man, woman and child seeks equal justice, equal opportunity, equal dignity without discrimination. Unless these rights have meaning there, they have little meaning anywhere. Without concerned citizen action to uphold them close to home, we shall look in vain for progress in the larger world."[61]

You can download information on the racial wealth gap including ideas on creating equitability, public policies like Baby Bonds, and a publication called "The Color of Wealth" by going to www.MattParadise.com/capablebonus.

# PART II

## MORE THAN TOUCHY-FEELY

The Psychology, Attitudes,
Behaviors, and Emotions of Money

# 6

# PAST MEMORIES, PRESENT DECISIONS, AND FUTURE HOPES

I've counseled and educated over 100,000 people and have found that psychology, emotion, and behavior have a significant impact on financial wellness: how we feel, why we decide what we do, and what's beneath the functional and dysfunctional relationships with money. These factors have a significant impact on our overall health and well-being. I've never met a single person who always makes the most rational, self-interested decisions.

Stressing over past mistakes and clinging to memories of how things used to be fills us with regret and can lead to depression and anxiety. We miss opportunities right in front of us. Managing painful or traumatic memories is important for our well-being. Healing from the past will help build a healthy and rich future.[62]

Riches aren't only about money. A financial asset is anything we own or control that can convert to cash. Money can buy things, but it's far from our most valuable resource. Time and health are our greatest assets, but they're often underappreciated until spent. If you trade all of your time for cash, you won't have any left for loved ones. Our investments influence the quality of our lives.

We can build whole health wealth by investing in the eight key areas of wellness: physical, emotional, intellectual, social, spiritual, environmental, occupational, and financial.[63] Wealthy people build and gain assets, while others, stuck in patterns of buying stuff and living beyond their means, have liabilities and poverty.

In my personal and professional experience, when we ignore psychology and mindset in our financial lives, it's to our own detriment. As we discuss building whole health wealth, we must consider behavior, knowledge, and access.

Consider how many armchair quarterbacks there are. It's easy to plan a passionate strategy on any given Sunday from the comfort of our homes. There is a dramatic difference between the critic and creator. Both may possess the same information, yet only one brings to life the mix of knowledge and skill, the wisdom gained through experience, and takes action. In managing our lives, we must learn, practice, and apply. This process takes discipline and self-control—and often overcoming obstacles that may seem insurmountable. The process is emotional. We all need grace when we miss the mark.

I've worked with many clients who lacked hope. When we lack hope, we rarely decide in the best interest of our future selves. I, personally, have a history with addiction. I harmed relationships, and I overdosed and nearly died in the ICU while loved ones watched with great sadness. Now, with over twenty years of sobriety, I know that well-being is more than not using. As Nobel Peace Prize–winning activist Desmond Tutu proclaimed, "Hope is being able to see that there is light despite all of the darkness."[64]

Do you have moments of hopelessness, fear, or worry? I guarantee it's possible to find hope in this hurting world. First, we can find help, comfort, and encouragement with peers, mentors, and professional counselors. Second, to regain hope, we must reframe our mindset. When we focus on things that are true and good and that we're grateful for, the peaceful, happy, and joyful moments will come more often. We don't need to forget the past; rather, we can embrace and learn from it. The choices we make today create our future.

## Memories Form Our Reality

Memories are powerful. They can change our perception of the world. Our memory can manipulate our current behaviors. Research shows that our emotions and feelings can have a significant impact on our financial choices.[65] Our relationships, language, and even our personal identity rely heavily upon our memory.

Memories involving money impact our financial behaviors.

- What is your first money memory?

- What was significant about the memory?

- What are the feelings that come to the surface as you recount the experience?

- How has the experience affected decisions you've made?

Here is one of my first money memories:

I was probably seven years old, and my younger brother was about four. We lived in a small house just outside Hartford, Connecticut. Since our cozy bedroom was too small for two beds, Ben and I had a trundle bed, which is a twin-sized bed with a mattress that lowers and slides under another twin bed. We thought it was the coolest thing.

It was the middle of the night when our mom woke us up. She explained we needed to help our father, whose car had broken down. Dad was an ironworker on the third shift. The overnight hours were grueling, but they provided a way to feed the family and keep a roof over our heads. I remember he had a small orange car. My mother followed his instructions and brought a nylon strap from the house to be used to tow the broken-down vehicle. I remember my dad attaching the strap to the front of his disabled car and connecting it to the rear of the family car. I remember the strap breaking multiple times as he attempted to get the cars home.

My young mind and time may have altered the memory, but this is how I remember the eventful night. Though, when it first occurred, I didn't think of it as a money memory.

My parents didn't speak about money very often. In hindsight, it's clear that they struggled financially. If they had had enough resources to keep two cars operable, they would have. If they had had a little extra cash, they certainly would have hired a tow truck rather than waking up their two young children in the middle of the night to tow a car.

I am incredibly grateful that my parents sacrificed for us. We didn't have everything we wanted, but we never went hungry (unless the food had onions in it, but that's a different story).

I remember feeling shame about getting picked up at school by my dad in his dirty jeans with holes, which exposed the protective kneepads underneath. I remember the jealousy and the longing for a shiny-penny life—one where money grew on trees, and both parents attended every soccer game and drove cars that never broke down in the middle of the night.

Context of family dynamics accompanies the memory of that one incident. I remember the hurt and grief caused by my maternal grandparents' derision as they perpetuated a narrative where my father was inadequate, less than, no good. He was, in their minds, the one who led their daughter to drop out of college and have a child out of wedlock. My grandparents had their own standards and opinions of how to build a successful life and family. Their views had an Anglo-Saxon veneer where every generation achieved greater and greater success built on privilege. There was irony in this perspective, since both of them were raised in poverty in rural Maine. I was told that my grandmother's childhood home had dirt floors.

My grandparents escaped their poor upbringing and worked to enter the upper class. My father's working-class rough hands and mixed race didn't fit their vision of a suitable husband for their daughter. And they vocalized their objections. It took years of patience and love for my dad to overcome their bigotry.

After reflection, I realized my parents maintained an illusion of plenty. My dad enjoyed buying new technology. My mom ensured there were lots of gifts for Christmas and birthdays. I call it an illusion because, like the example of the broken car, there wasn't always money to pay for necessities. Their budget did not always balance. My grandparents subsidized our lives.

My first money memory has affected financial decisions throughout my life in positive and negative ways. I have been fiercely independent, and my stubbornness and poor choices left me homeless. I avoided student and auto debt, but struggled to pay rent and buy food while earning below the poverty line. The fear of living in a cycle of poverty motivated choices and because of that fear, I've made many mistakes. The fear also motivated me to overcome homelessness and build a career, helping people avoid and rise above financial struggles.

Multigenerational poverty cycles are extremely difficult to break. Family poverty can traumatize survivors for generations. Healing of past trauma is necessary to build a healthy future. I'm grateful that we don't have to be defined by our past.

We cannot change our past. We can, however, understand how our individual and collective pasts influence who we are today. And we can change. And we can create change for our loved ones. You may not have a drug addiction, but you may relate to having a lack of hope.

Let me be clear. There is hope. I've helped others and have received help through challenging times and have learned a valuable lesson: we need each other.

The Holocaust survivor, Nobel Prize recipient, and human rights activist Elie Wiesel said, "Just as man cannot live without dreams, he cannot live without hope. If dreams reflect the past, hope summons the future . . . Because I remember, I despair. Because I remember, I have the duty to reject despair . . . Just as despair can come to one only from other human beings, hope too can be given to one only by other human beings."[66]

# MONEY TALK Q&A

Q: Where can I learn more about memories and decision making?

A: Here are a few helpful recommendations

- *The Memory Illusion: Remembering, Forgetting, and the Science of False Memory* by Dr. Julia Shaw

- Money Memories Podcast (https://www.npr.org /podcasts/947650726/money-memories)

- *A Mind for Numbers: How to Excel at Math and Science* by Barbara Oakley, PhD

If you're interested in an academic deep dive, *Nature Human Behavior, Current Opinion in Behavioral Sciences,* the *Journal of Behavioral Decision Making,* and the *Journal of Financial Therapy* are treasure troves of peer-reviewed research. You can enter your search word(s) of choice, including money memory.

- https://www.nature.com/nathumbehav/

- https://www.sciencedirect.com/journal /current-opinion-in-behavioral-sciences

- https://onlinelibrary.wiley.com/journal/10990771

- https://newprairiepress.org/jft/

For more inspiration, information, and a free First Money Memory worksheet go to www.MattParadise.com/capablebonus.

# 7

## WHAT DO YOU VALUE?

### Personal, Cultural, and Financial Values

The Patriots are the greatest football team, and Tom Brady is the best quarterback ever. I realize that, for some of you, these are fighting words. Other readers may not care about sports at all. We all have different beliefs, values, and aspirations. This is one significant reason personal finance is so, well, PERSONAL.

There are some basic common principles, but the decisions of each family vary significantly. These decisions are far less about right and wrong choices, and more about what's most beneficial for the individual household.

Family, friends, environment, and culture influences our beliefs, values, thoughts, and attitudes. We must have our own personal convictions so we don't become directionless and subject to fluctuating emotions or negative influence from others. In a consumer-driven economy, that means marketers, retailers, and profit-driven companies will steer you toward what they believe is best. Direction determines destiny.

We must each ask ourselves, "What do I value and how are they prioritized in my financial plan?"

At one end of the financial spectrum, we have people who intentionally subject themselves to humble lives of service. If we measured their lives by financial wealth, we'd consider them poor and might harshly judge them as failures. A life well lived is the sum of so much more than the amount of money someone died with.

Our life experiences help shape our personal values. Our values, principles, and what we consider worthwhile motivate and fulfill us. They help us define the significance of various actions. It's not right or wrong to value family over career advancement or walks in nature over listening to music. Over time, our values often change. Now that I am in my forties, the ways I spend my resources, such as time, energy, and money, are much different from when I was in my teens or twenties.

## Customs and Traditions (What's Your Way of Life?)

Besides our personal values, there are also societal values. In the United States, freedom is a value granted in the nation's founding documents. The Declaration of Independence, Constitution, and Bill of Rights comprise the Charters of Freedom, which are instrumental to the country's founding and philosophy.

This freedom allows Americans to express individualism (though there's a lot of work before we have "justice for all"). There are cultures in the world where collectivist culture thrives. In these communities, the health and well-being of the entire group is more valuable than individual wants and desires. As an example, some cultures use community kitchens and shared water sources. Some consider personal saving as hoarding resources and a selfish act.

Over fifteen years ago, I had the honor of marrying into a Chinese family. My wife's upbringing was psychologically, emotionally, culturally, and materially different from my childhood. I'm not claiming that one culture is better or above the other. They are, in reality, simply different.

I moved out of my parents' house around the age of sixteen. I estranged myself from family and didn't value the relationships. In contrast, there is an expectation in the culture of my wife's family that children will sacrifice to care for their parents. Traditionally, this has been the responsibility of the oldest son. My wife has one younger sister and no brothers, so the duty of taking care of her aging parents fell on her.

As I embraced different cultural values, my personal values and perspective about family dramatically changed. I've mended broken connections with my family and embraced my in-laws. My wife and I consider caring for her parents our responsibility, and we have sacrificed and planned our lives accordingly. We have an addition on our house so that we can provide care as they continue to age.

Here are a few other cultural examples to consider. In North America, we're familiar with the concept of a lemonade stand. Maybe you've visited one. The idea is simple: kids set up a table and sell paper or plastic cups filled with beverages in their front yard. Through the activity, children learn economic concepts such as supply and demand, scarcity and choice, and market value. They learn business and skills, such as cash flow, income, and budgeting.

In American culture, we commonly encourage the entrepreneurial spirit. Some cultures consider teaching personal finance to children inappropriate. I once taught a group of young children and their caregivers. Most were excited to have some basic financial education and counseling. One grandmother passionately opposed the idea of teaching children about money. She said, "In my culture, money is for adults to be concerned with. The role of a child is to play and learn. They can learn about finances when they're older." She was an immigrant, and her viewpoint was culturally different from that of the rest of the group.

It's not my role to change someone's value system. My goal is to help illuminate realities through education so that individuals and families can make informed decisions about the lives they're building.

For some individuals and families, remittances account for a large part of the household budget. A remittance, in this context, is when someone working in the United States electronically transfers money to friends or family living out of the country. If you were born in the US, it's possible that you've never heard of or thought of the idea. It's not within our culture.

## Beyond Belief

Religion plays a significant role in many people's lives. Some religious individuals and families contribute 10% or more of their income to their faith community. There are various reasons someone might contribute such a large sum. Some may consider the giving a duty or an act of obedience. Some may consider the money a wise investment into their community. Others may consider giving an expression of thanksgiving or joy.

In our house, we contribute to our church and other charities for several reasons. One personal reason is that we're giving to God out of an expression of love. We give to help promote social, racial, and economic justice. More valuable than money, we also give our hearts and time. We provide mentorship, volunteer with multiple nonprofits, and collect and distribute food to households who are food insecure.

Is spirituality important to you? Either way, it's a choice. Aligning values with how we spend our resources is a step toward well-being. When our time, effort, energy, lifestyle, and money align with personal values, we are content.

What do you value? To help understand and identify personal values, the social psychologist Shalom Schwartz developed the Theory of Basic Human Values.[67] People from around the world have found his survey helpful while on the journey of self-exploration. You can find free human values tests based on Schwartz's work to evaluate how people from different cultures prioritize ten universal human values on the Financially Capable bonus page.

As your list develops, you'll likely notice that some items are more important to you than others. Make a note of your personal values so you can prioritize them.

What do you consider a life well lived? Think about your goals, principles, feelings, and activities. Ask yourself: What am I becoming? What am I working toward? What kind of life am I building?

It's helpful to periodically review what's important to us. My principles and values have radically changed over the years, and I work to align my goals and day-to-day activities with them. My wife and I have similar values; we prioritize faith and family. We've sacrificed time, personal comfort, and money to align our lifestyle with these values. Though this isn't always easy, our lives are infinitely richer and happier. We use our values as both a barometer and a compass.

Disparities between what we value and how we live our lives create discontentment, frustration, and despair. Negative emotions can lead to dysfunctional behavior. We have the power to change our mindset to align personal values and choices. Aligning ideals, hopes, and actions leads to whole health wealth.

# MONEY TALK Q&A

## Q: How can I find out my money type values?

A: Most people are some combination of the following types:

- Rational: Tends to make most decisions by the numbers
- Idealist: Tends to care less about money than other goals
- Guardian: Tends to be cautious with money
- Artisan: Tends to be freewheeling and daring

You can take a free CNN money type quiz here: http://cnnmon.ie/2a6OgqU.

For more helpful resources about values, including instant access to a free human values test, go to www.MattParadise.com/capablebonus.

# 8

# HEALTHY RELATIONSHIPS LEAD TO A RICH LIFE AND ADDICTIONS MAKE US POOR

My sweet tooth has motivated me like a kid in a candy store. I've driven out of my way for a delicious dessert. There's nothing quite like the unbridled giddiness caused by the neural reward in the prefrontal cortex when the taste of sugar triggers dopamine and hormones that tell our bodies, "Mmmmm, this is good!" The chemical structure $C_{12}H_{22}O_{11}$, a.k.a. sugar, can be incredibly addictive.

Spending money can also be incredibly addictive. According to research, "there's actually a lot of psychological and therapeutic value when you're shopping. Even window shopping or online browsing can bring brain-fueled happiness."[68] For some people, shopping activates the release of dopamine, a brain chemical that brings a sense of euphoria. The practice even has a name: retail therapy.

I've counseled tens of thousands of people who bought into the idea that purchases would provide emotional relief. More often than not, I've seen the practice result in shame, remorse, and high-interest debt. This dysfunctional and emotional cycle of overspending is difficult to break. Managing money involves far more than dollars and cents. It also requires healthy behaviors and attitudes.

Consider your first thoughts and emotions when you contemplate shopping. You're not alone if you don't picture rehab or destroyed relationships. Do you have a different picture in your mind when you hear cocaine or heroin? Please don't take the idea out of context. I'm not saying that retail therapy is the same as using narcotics, nor am I minimizing the pain caused by drug abuse. I'm a lucky survivor of a drug overdose and am all too familiar with the damage caused by addictive behaviors.

Habits like overspending, gambling, and accumulating debt have addictive properties. Consider this definition of addiction: "A condition in which a person engages in the use of a substance or in a behavior for which the rewarding effects provide a compelling incentive to repeatedly pursue the behavior despite detrimental consequences."[69]

Negative thoughts about money are so pervasive that they become part of us. We may think that "money is the root of all evil." I speak from experience. I slept on floors for years because a mattress was too expensive, and my self-worth plummeted. This became a vicious cycle of destructive behavior and poor decisions. Depression dominated my life and bills piled up.

Sometimes (okay, often) I felt as if I needed an escape from the realities and challenges of life. If eating out soothed me, then that was easy to justify. Going to the movies one more time in the month, or buying a gift for someone, or one more taxi ride (this was during the time I rode my bike two miles each way to work) didn't seem to matter. The expenses weren't bad; however, I was living above my means and got into credit card debt.

From an economic point of view, we encourage spending money. Our economy receives a generous boost from over-spending. In 2008, the Bush administration sent out stimulus checks and encouraged unplanned shopping to battle the reces-sion. Economics and personal finance are two different topics. Some behaviors are beneficial for the economy but detrimental for an individual.

Households cannot spend their way out of debt. I've seen dysfunctional behaviors cause tremendous destruction. I remember counseling one family with $500,000 in credit card debt. Yes, you read that correctly—half a million bucks. The amount didn't include the additional student loans and secured debt like cars and a mortgage. The family had been making the minimum payment on the revolving debt for years. At 25% to 30% APR, they were treading water and didn't make a dent in their principal balances. (I'll cover interest rates and debt man-agement strategies in Part III of this book.) They were beyond stressed.

## Consider Self-Control as a Money Issue

Financial education is useless without a solid grasp of financial behavior. All the knowledge in the world won't overcome a lack of self-control. In a culture of excess, dysfunctional relationships with money surround us and "The American Dream" becomes a materialistic nightmare. The shame of poverty and failing to meet other people's expectations for our lives is painful. Comparing our house, job, clothes, accomplishments, bank account, etc., with our neighbors, or worse, images on TV and social media, creates an unhealthy tsunami of emotion.

Here are sentiments from some of my clients that might resonate with you: "I have more bills than I can afford. Forget the bills, I'm going shopping." "I don't know what the interest rates are. I stopped opening the mail because it's only full of more bad news." "I'm so stressed about money that I can barely function." "I wish I learned about money in school; now it's too late."

Pretending to be rich is often the pathway to poverty. Don't get me wrong; money is for spending. Shopping is necessary for a healthy economy. Consumer spending helps businesses invest and grow. Jobs in every sector of the economy rely on businesses doing well. As consumers, we must buy food, purchase clothes, and live in apartments and houses. It's possible to have a healthy relationship with money and purchase luxuries. When we seek ongoing comfort through spending and neglect necessities, dysfunction becomes a habit.

Spending money isn't a bad thing. Money is just a tool, and how we use it makes all the difference. A healthy relationship with money includes financial literacy and an understanding of behavioral economics. We must understand how psychological, cognitive, emotional, cultural, and social factors impact the financial decisions we make.

## Consider Health a Money Issue

There are direct connections between finances and overall health. Health is wealth and wealth is health. "Low wealth is a risk factor that can dynamically change over a person's life and can influence a person's cardiovascular health status."[70] Harvard Medical School researchers draw an important distinction between income and wealth. It's quite possible to have a high income with a negative net worth by carrying debt. And debt can be stressful.

I can confirm that living in poverty is stressful. Healthy foods are expensive, worry and anxiety can affect sleep, and poor sleep and diet combined are a recipe for an unhealthy cycle. Poverty creates physiological changes. Financial stress and poverty affect cognitive function, according to the authors of the book *Scarcity*. Sendhil Mullainathan and Eldar Shafir show that scarcity creates a distinct psychology for everyone struggling to manage with less than they need. The book illustrates how individuals and organizations can better manage scarcity for greater satisfaction and success.[71] Healthy financial relationships require more than manifesting a positive attitude. They take knowledge, discipline, and often a helping hand.

## Addictions Make Building Wealth Difficult

Addiction affects every family in the United States. It's estimated that 30% of Americans have suffered from an alcohol use disorder alone. That's close to 100 million people.[72]

In addition to more well-known drug addictions, there are also process, or behavioral, addictions. When someone compulsively engages in a rewarding non-drug-related behavior despite negative consequences, they may have a behavioral addiction; for example, compulsive shopping, excessive gambling, or greed.

Data collected from 83 studies found that up to 61% of US adults have an addiction. According to the research, half of the US adult population suffers from an addictive disorder.[73]

Take a moment for some serious self-reflection while considering these questions. It can be helpful to journal your thoughts and feelings.

- Have your spending habits, alcohol, or drug use negatively affected one or more relationships?

- Have you shopped, gotten drunk, or used drugs in order to forget about a personal problem?

- Has your work or school performance ever suffered because of spending, drinking or drug use?

- Do you feel the urge to go shopping when you're feeling down or depressed?

- Do you feel guilt after impulse purchases?

- Are you living on the edge of financial stability but still make impulse purchases (barely paying rent or bills, for example)?

- Are your credit cards almost to their limit or maxed out?

- Do you feel a lack of contentment or an unrestrained desire for more than you need?

Addictions are difficult topics to discuss. The destruction caused by ignoring dysfunctional behaviors is real. The consequences include reduced physical, mental, social, and financial well-being. A professional counselor may be helpful if you or a loved one have signs of addictive behavior. A "money guru" may not be sufficient.

I've heard too many well-intentioned financial professionals offer blanket statement advice. This can damage and even traumatize a person. Maybe you've heard this advice: "Just stop spending more than you're making and everything will be okay." Or, "Just work harder/more hours." Yes, balanced spending plans are important. However, ignoring root causes of financial disfunction, disregarding health and well-being, and only focusing on financial spreadsheets won't create whole health wealth.

## When Spending Becomes Unhealthy

Spending becomes unhealthy when an individual pathologically pursues reward and relief they can't afford while disregarding the consequences. This can lead to financial destruction and ruined relationships. It's difficult to identify unhealthy spending habits, particularly in a consumer-based society. One group that works to combat the negative effects of dysfunctional money management is Spenders Anonymous. The group is a community of people sharing experiences, strength, and encouragement while working toward clarity in their relationship with money.

Similar to Alcoholics Anonymous (AA), Spenders Anonymous has a 12-step program. You can find resources and personal stories on their website: www.spenders.org. There are also groups to help work through the addictions of gambling and incurring unsecured debt. You can find information and local groups on their respective websites: www.gamblersanonymous .org and www.debtorsanonymous.org.

When we're overwhelmed with the compulsion to spend money, it's helpful to stop and take a moment to consider our actions. It's more challenging to be in control when we're *hungry, angry, lonely*, or *tired*. You might recognize that these four words create the acronym HALT.

Remove temptation. I had a client who literally put her credit cards on ice. Jazmyne put her cards in a bag filled with water and put everything in the freezer. Every time she had the urge to go shopping, the extra step of thawing the ice gave her time to reconsider and center herself to a state of calm. The strategy worked for her and she became debt-free.

Our world is full of stress. Learning to manage stress is a central component to building whole health wealth. Some people wield money wisely and accomplish tremendous goals. Others squander resources or become consumed with greed and the sentiment that more is never enough. Increasing our awareness about personal decisions, large and small, allows us to develop mastery and be in control of the lives we're building.

Many emotions are associated with money. When we realize our financial values and control our behaviors, we are well on our way to a functional relationship with money and a wealthy life.

# MONEY TALK Q&A

## Q: What help is there if I don't have an addiction but I still need help to build a healthy relationship with money?

A: A transformational book to consider is *The Soul of Money: Transforming Your Relationship with Money and Life* by Lynne Twist.

Another influential book is *The Psychology of Money: Timeless Lessons on Wealth, Greed, and Happiness* by Morgan Housel.

If you need help to identify destructive behaviors and address root causes of financial stress, explore these recommendations:

- Debtors Anonymous (https://debtorsanonymous.org/)

- Spenders Anonymous (www.spenders.org/)

- Gamblers Anonymous (www.gamblersanonymous.org /ga/)

## Q: Where can I go to learn more about financial psychology?

A: Here are a couple of free resources:

- Center for Advanced Hindsight (https://advanced -hindsight.com/course/a-beginners-guide-to-irrational -behavior-via-coursera/)

- Class Central (https://www.classcentral.com/course /duke-behavioral-finance-6635)

## Q: Where can I get help for my financial dysfunction?

A: Money-related stress, compulsivity, addiction(s), poverty, loss of income and/or assets, and differing habits or values from a loved one can all come with complicated emotions. Some people who experience financial challenges benefit from working with a mental health professional.

National Alliance on Mental Illness (https://namimainline pa.org/choosing-the-right-mental-health-professional/) provides some direction in choosing the best professional for your situation.

Cognitive-behavioral therapy can be helpful: https://positive psychology.com/cbt-cognitive-behavioral-therapy.

For suggested reading, resources, and recommendations for free behavioral economics courses, go to www.MattParadise.com/capablebonus.

# PART III

## NUTS AND BOLTS

The Fundamental Knowledge of
Financial Literacy

# 9

# WHY ISN'T FINANCIAL EDUCATION TAUGHT IN SCHOOLS?

Perhaps you've heard less-than-helpful advice such as "Don't spend more than you make." "Student loans and mortgages are always good debt." Or the crowd favorite, "If you stop buying avocado toast and lattés and invest the money, you'll be richer than Jeff Bezos."

While spending less than we make is good practice, advice that lacks empathy, understanding, or specificity can have a discouraging effect.

The first part of this book is about access and opportunity within our financial environment. The second section addresses the psychology, attitudes, behaviors, and emotions of money. In this third and final part of the book, I'll get into financial information, some facts and figures, data and statistics. For some of you, this may be the part where your eyes glaze over in discussions about IRAs, 401(k)s, compounding interest, credit scores, and numbers. Other readers may get excited about the topics and dream of the wealth they're going to build.

Financial literacy helps us to understand the math, while action and discipline allow us to leverage the knowledge to grow wealth. I began investing in the stock market when I was twenty. My contributions were small, but the slow and steady strategy has done well. Over the years, I have had many opportunities to join get-rich-quick schemes. While working at American Consumer Credit Counseling, I actually had one of our auditors call me with an offer to join him in a networking marketing business. Fortunately, I recognized the venture as a shady pyramid scheme and declined his offer.

## Don't Overcomplicate Learning

E. O. Wilson, author and biologist known for developing the field of sociobiology, said, "We are drowning in information but starved for knowledge."[74] This was well before the internet and more volumes of information than we can count. For financial data, the quote rings true today. There's arguably too much information available. Have you gotten lost in or overwhelmed by opinions about money management, saving, investing, and similar topics?

I suffer from analysis paralysis, which is when someone overthinks a problem without taking decisive action. It's easy to spend an hour or more diving into a Google spiral. My car ran out of windshield washer fluid, so I did an online search for the best performance for the best price. Now, there were many other ways I could have spent the time, but pursuing information is addicting. I read the ingredients of various fluids, which led me to efficacy, which led me to learning about various scientific properties. You may shake your head in disbelief like my wife did, or nod with complete understanding. Either way, sellers love when we travel down this rabbit hole. The deeper we dive, the more likely we are to spend money. In economics, this is called *sunk cost*. The irrational behavior describes our tendency to follow through on an endeavor if we have already invested time, effort, or money into it, whether or not the current costs outweigh the benefits.[75]

You can spend the rest of your life pursuing financial information. My goal is to provide you with actionable knowledge. I have found a "learn, apply, grow" cycle is helpful for reaching goals. As soon as we're proficient in one area, the environment changes. Finance laws change, products and services change, our perspectives and goals change. The pursuit of knowledge is an ongoing cycle.

You may have heard terms like *personal finance, financial literacy, financial education, financial capability,* and *financial well-being* used interchangeably. Personal finance is different from business finance, although you may get your household income from your own business. Please, please keep the two separate. Since this book focuses on personal finance, we won't get into business details.

- **Personal finance** focuses on the basic principles and methods we use to get income and manage assets.

- **Financial literacy** involves possessing the knowledge to make informed judgments about managing resources. This is different from financial education. We teach students reading, writing, and arithmetic. The teaching alone doesn't mean they're proficient in a subject.

- **Financial capability** is the combination of knowledge, behavior, and opportunity. Every year, students graduate from schools, many of which provide exceptional education. An advanced degree may show understanding, but it doesn't qualify an individual as capable. Some employers treat graduates with an MBA like they're a dime a dozen. Students graduate with tremendous knowledge about theory, but often lack practical knowledge. A graduate degree in nutritional science does not make an individual healthy.

- **Financial well-being** is a barometer of how one feels regarding their finances. It is highly subjective.

Let's explore some data that show how important financial education really is.

- A *Fortune* magazine study of 27,564 Americans found that nearly two-thirds of the participants couldn't pass a basic test of financial literacy. Their lack of knowledge was also clear in the participants' financial behavior.

- *Forbes* also found that 44% of Americans don't have enough cash to cover a $400 emergency, 43% of student loan borrowers are not making payments, and 38% of US households have credit card debt. On average, American adults owe $16,048 with an APR of 16.47%, and 33% have $0 saved for retirement.[76]

The National Foundation for Credit Counseling (NFCC) surveyed people throughout the country and found these startling numbers:

- Three out of five Americans don't maintain a budget. Only two of every five say they have a budget and keep close track of how much they spend on such things as food, housing, and entertainment.

- Six out of ten adults have had credit card debt in the past twelve months, and nearly two in five say their household carries this debt from month to month.

- Fewer than one in five US adults are very confident about their retirement savings; one in four are not confident at all. And, when asked what areas of personal finance worry them most, the top response continues to be retiring and not having enough money set aside.[77]

After a while we can get lost in the numbers. Why do I bother? The need for financial education is clear. We need it, and in the United States we're severely lacking in it.

You might ask, "Don't they teach personal finance in schools?" The answer mostly is no. This is coming from my personal experience of teaching personal finance in schools and also examining national data. States remain inconsistent in the quality of delivery, since there is no federal standard for financial education.

NextGen Personal Finance conducted a nationwide study of 12 million students across 12,000 high schools and found only one in four students actually receive required financial education. For students attending schools with low-income students or Students who are Black and Brown, the number drops to one in twenty.[78] During the 2022 legislative session, lawmakers in twenty-five states and the District of Columbia introduced bills which would require schools to provide financial education. While educational requirements are helpful, they do not guarantee high-quality programs. Our goal is to ensure that graduating students are financially capable.

Standard & Poor's Global Financial Literacy Survey ranks the United States fourteenth when measuring the proportion of adults in the country who are financially literate. Let's do a quick comparison. The US adult financial literacy level, at

57%, is only slightly higher than that of Botswana, whose economy is 1,127% smaller.[79]

Given the billions of dollars spent on financial education, one might think that our financial literacy levels are increasing. Sadly, the opposite is true. The Financial Industry Regulatory Authority (FINRA) discovered a clear decline in financial literacy over the past twelve years in its "State of US Financial Capability" study. Fewer than half of the surveyed adults correctly answered four or more questions about fundamental concepts of economics and personal finance.[80] You can see how your state ranks and also test yourself here: www.usfinancialcapability.org.

Not all is lost. FINRA data show that when people receive more financial education—over ten hours—they spend less money than they earn. It might sound like common sense, but the more financial knowledge we have, the more literate we are, which leads to greater financial capability and increased financial wellness.

My encouragement is simple: continue to learn and share your wisdom. Beware, there is a danger in learning just a little. Many people act on their overconfident feelings. Social media are full of get-rich-quick schemes. Don't get me wrong—while scrolling across social media, I've been entertained, made fantastic connections, and learned all kinds of things. Let's put it this way: if I were going to build a house, I wouldn't want the foundation poured by someone whose only experience was watching a few TikToks or Reels.

# MONEY TALK Q&A

## Q: Really, though. Why isn't personal finance taught in schools?

A: Schools offer it, but the content quality varies significantly. Most states have at least a basic personal finance standard or requirement in public school. On the other end of the spectrum, only a handful of states require a full stand-alone personal finance course in high school. Education legislation continues to change and you can help.

## Q: How can I advocate for financial education?

A: I think of advocacy on multiple levels, no one greater than the other. In thinking about legislative action, there is work on the federal, state, and local levels. The JumpStart Coalition (www .jumpstart.org/) is one nonprofit organization working on all levels to advance financial literacy, particularly in public schools.

To access more data and resources and to get involved, check out the Council for Economic Education (www.council foreconed.org), National Association of State Treasurers (https:// nast.org/financialwellness/census/), and Next Gen Personal Finance (www.ngpf.org/expand-access/).

For more education than you'll find on your Instagram feed, including research on financial literacy in schools and how to get involved in your neighborhood, go to www.MattParadise.com/capablebonus.

# 10

## MOVING BEYOND BASIC

When I tell someone that I'm in the business of financial education, their assumption is that I sell financial services and products. Let's consider the financial services industry through the lens of the Consumer Financial Protection Bureau (CFPB). The CFPB is a US government agency "dedicated to making sure you are treated fairly by banks, lenders and other financial institutions."

The bureau found that the financial services industry spends approximately $17 billion each year marketing products and services to consumers. Meanwhile, companies spend only $670 million annually to provide "education" to consumers. This spending translates to about $54 per person on marketing, while only $2 is spent educating us.[81]

Those numbers highlight the need for consumers to access unbiased information. We are aware of products like loans, but we may not have knowledge about details and their true cost.

So what does this mean? It means that financial institutions provide just enough "education" to sound helpful, but their goal is to prompt consumers to buy their products and services. The US government, through the CFPB, provides this insight: "The significant disparity in resources devoted to financial education as opposed to marketing financial services underscores the importance of providing high-quality sources of unbiased financial information to consumers."[82] Marketing is not selfless teaching. We would be foolish to believe that tobacco and vape industry-sponsored school-based prevention programs are in the best interest of children. When a lender "teaches" how to use a loan, it's likely marketing, not education.

Marketing serves to bias consumers. Businesses are well aware of behavioral economics and use the concept to maximize profit. It can be extremely difficult to sort out fact from fiction. Not only do institutions market well, they also influence rules and regulations for their industry.

Open Secrets is a nonpartisan, independent nonprofit organization. It's run by the Center for Responsive Politics, which is the nation's premier research group tracking money in US politics and its effect on elections and public policy. They reported the total spent lobbying Congress on behalf of finance, insurance, and real estate industries in 2022 alone was over $600 million. There were 2,450 lobbyists. Of those employed/contracted, more than half, 60.74%, were former government employees. We may consider some of this work a conflict of interest for the American people.[83]

Between legislators and lobbyists exists a practice called a revolving door. This is the common practice of government regulators, congressional staff, and even members of Congress to take new jobs with lobbying firms and private-sector organizations that, in many cases, they used to oversee. Those who go the other direction, from private sector to positions in the government, are sometimes called "reverse revolvers."

The point is that sometimes legislators go to work for the very firms we elected them to regulate. That hardly seems unbiased.

## BANKruptcy helps who?

When I worked in the credit counseling industry, part of my job was to stay on top of legislation. Bankruptcy is huge in the debt management world. I remember several years ago when there was significant lobbying to reform bankruptcy laws.

The resulting legislation was the Bankruptcy Abuse Prevention and Consumer Protection Act of 2005. One significant change in the law made it much more difficult for consumers to file for chapter 7 bankruptcy. Using this section of bankruptcy code, people can discharge or get rid of debts. This is in contrast to chapter 11, where the court arranges repayment of debt.[84]

Before the reform, it was easy for bankruptcy filers to have their debt wiped clean. Now, a "means test" is required. The test determines if a filer can pay anything toward their debt, and it forces many into chapter 11.

Many consumer advocates and professionals failed to see clear consumer benefits in the reform. Bankruptcy judge Keith M. Lundin of Tennessee said, "Unquestionably, this is the most poorly written piece of legislation that I or anyone else has ever seen."[85]

The then-president of the National Association of Consumer Bankruptcy Attorneys, Henry J. Sommer, said that the 2005 amendments were not helping or protecting consumers. He said the reform caused an enormous increase in bankruptcy filing costs and burdens.[86]

Michael Simkovic, a former fellow at Harvard's John M. Olin Center for Law and Economics, wrote, "The data suggests that although bankruptcies and credit card company losses decreased, and credit card companies achieved record profits, the cost to consumers of credit card debt actually increased."[87]

Therefore, the 2005 bankruptcy reforms benefited large businesses at consumers' expense. *BusinessWeek* reporter Christopher Farrell said, "A law intended to help the financial industry may be damaging the housing sector, creditors and borrowers alike." For you history buffs, all of this preceded the Great Recession in 2007–2009.[88]

## "Too big to fail"

You may remember terms like *credit crunch* and *crisis*. The Great Recession was a horrible time. Many Americans lost their jobs and homes while big banks received bailouts. They were deemed "too big to fail."

I'll discuss predatory practices and products a bit later, but it's important to distinguish the difference between sales and education. This isn't about bank-bashing. There are great financial institutions with community-building at their heart. Some bank managers realize that helping consumers is good for the bottom line as well. Profit is paramount for the survival of any business; however, some companies put profit above all else.

This behavior has shown itself to be dangerous. The history of AIG is one example. AIG, American International Group, Inc., is one of the largest finance and insurance companies. This global firm had about $1 trillion in assets prior to the crisis and lost $99.2 billion in 2008.

On September 16 2008, the Federal Reserve Bank of New York stepped in with an $85 billion loan to keep the failing company from going under. Though the reasons for the significant losses that AIG suffered are fuzzy, a couple of commonly accepted areas are to blame. One practice that caused tremendous losses was securities lending. AIG lost $21 billion in securities lending, though this lending wasn't discussed as much during the crisis.

Executives at AIG overvalued the securities. AIG received their bailout from the government and then rewarded employees with huge bonuses totaling hundreds of millions of dollars. Representative Paul Hodes (Democrat, New Hampshire) said, "I think AIG now stands for arrogance, incompetence and greed."[89]

The company's credit default swaps/collateralized debt obligations (CDOs) were widely accepted to have contributed significantly to their collapse. Institutional investors bought popular and complicated CDOs, financial products that lump together loans and other assets.

CDOs are "collateralized" assets because the promised repayments of the underlying assets are the collateral that gives the CDOs their value. The pooled assets range in quality. For instance, mortgage-backed securities have subprime loans, which are loans for poor credit, as well as loans from well-qualified borrowers. The companies who rated the assets, such as Moody's Investors Service, complicated the safety of investing in these assets.

Dozens of lawsuits alleged that the credit rating agencies misrepresented the risk in these complicated products. The behavior of the institutions led to some of the biggest financial reform in US history. In 2010, the federal government enacted the Dodd-Frank Wall Street Reform and Consumer Protection Act. The act provided widespread reform to the regulatory system and provided significant protections for consumers. For example, it created a new agency, the CFPB, and tasked it with consumer protection.[90]

It's important that we understand personal finance within the context of the economy and learn from mistakes. To paraphrase an adage: if we don't learn from the past, we're doomed to repeat it.

## Selling vs. Teaching

We discussed how primary school financial education is lacking. For all the money a student pays for college, there must be some great life skills taught there. Right? Higher education does not provide the information for graduate success in personal financial matters. In fact, the US Financial Literacy and Education Commission wrote a report in 2019 recommending that institutions of higher education make financial literacy courses mandatory.

In their financial literacy best practices for higher education, the Commission suggested this: "The cost of higher education can be difficult to understand because of the lack of consistency and transparency in the information provided to potential students, and the inherent challenge to comprehend long-term implications of borrowing. The difficulty may be compounded due to lack of relevant, transparent, and timely information."[91]

So, to clarify, the government, which underwrites financial aid for colleges, itself says that the information provided for students to be successful is confusing. In the worst cases, the information provided to students is incorrect and irrelevant. That's problematic.

College students need their education to be relevant. A 2022 survey of students' personal finance realities showed the necessity for stronger financial literacy education and support. One in five don't know how much debt they'll have at graduation, and the half who know the amount do not know what their approximate payment will be. It's bad enough to graduate with student loans. An even greater challenge is to have student loans without a degree. Many students need to leave college to afford to live.

One-quarter of students said they've experienced food insecurity during college and 17 percent have dealt with housing insecurity; two-thirds work at least part time, with one in five working at least 30 hours per week.[92]

I've taught personal finance in Ivy League colleges and found that even students with multiple advanced degrees lacked basic financial knowledge and understanding of our banking system.

## Be the Change

While we won't create an academic utopia overnight, we can make a difference today. We can read and take personal finance courses. I've found that better education and overall well-being starts with looking in the mirror. When we become financially capable and employ an "each one teach one" mentality, we can create genuine change. We can speak up and advocate for better legislation. We can help loved ones increase their financial abilities. We can volunteer in our communities and help empower others.

A few years ago, my team organized an event to bring service providers together to help military veterans and service members with budgeting, debt management, retirement planning, and more.

To make the event possible, I worked with the Office of State Treasurer and received a grant to buy food, rent tables, and pay for the space at a local community college. Besides the grant, the treasurer also sent a couple of employees from the Unclaimed Property Division.

If you're not familiar with Unclaimed Property, this information might be well worth the price of this book. When financial institutions have abandoned property such as uncashed checks, security deposits, or overpayments, they attempt to contact the owner. If their attempts are unsuccessful, the institutions then turn over the assets to state or local government. There are billions of dollars waiting for the owners to claim them. States receive more than $3 billion annually.

If you're wondering if you have money waiting for you, consider that one in ten people in the US has money in a government account waiting to be claimed. By law, every state (and some provinces in Canada) has a free program to search for and claim the money. Don't get duped into paying for a service. Be sure to check with each state you've ever been associated with. Check places where you lived, worked, or even had family.

You can go directly to your state's official government site or check here: https://unclaimed.org/. What are you waiting for? Even if you don't find money, be sure to tell your friends and family.

One particular active duty service member, Juan, came to the event overwhelmed and stressed about his finances. He, like many people, had credit card debt, and during some months had trouble paying his monthly expenses and saving any money.

He was short on time to focus on money, since he had a duty to God and country that came before his personal finances. With encouragement, Juan reluctantly visited the State Treasurer's booth and allowed them to check for any abandoned property.

Are you sitting down? Juan had just over $18,000 that he wasn't aware of. The financial institution had tried to reach him, but because of the military relocations, Juan hadn't received their communications. The government was patiently waiting for the money to be claimed. It overwhelmed Juan with excitement, joy, and embarrassment.

For Juan and many others, the quick, free search had an enormous impact. Sometimes I get frustrated that information like this isn't more widely accessed. Shouldn't the government find people to reunite them with their long lost dollars? During these times, I realize I need to take a deep breath, chill out, and remind myself that at least Juan found help.

It's overwhelming to consider all the problems in the world. Rather than give up on the good that can be done, it's worthwhile to remember that helping one person can make a significant difference. Education is powerful and can alter the trajectory of a life and family. After all, as author Leo Buscaglia said, "Change is the end result of all true learning."[93] In order to change and effect change, let's continue learning.

# MONEY TALK Q&A

Q: Math can be difficult for some people. Where can I go for help with complicated financial calculations?

A: Online calculators are extremely helpful. I like Bankrate (https://www.bankrate.com/calculators.aspx).

Q: Where can I find more personal finance-related resources?

A: Some trustworthy resources include these:

- My Money (https://www.mymoney.gov/)
- National Endowment for Financial Education (research & advocacy focused) (https://www.nefe.org/)
- Federal Deposit Insurance Corporation (https://www .fdic.gov/resources/consumers/money-smart/)
- National Credit Union Administration (https://www .ncua.gov/consumers/financial-literacy-resources)
- Investopedia (https://www.investopedia.com/)
- Consumer Financial Protection Bureau (https://www .consumerfinance.gov/)
- American Institute of CPAs (https://www.360financial literacy.org/)

For more money tips including how to search for unclaimed property for free, visit www.MattParadise.com/capablebonus.

# 11

# THAT DIRTY B WORD

Estimated expenses, allowance, spending plan, ration, personal statement, budgetary figures, cost of operation, resource planning, allocation of expenditures—these are the many ways to describe what the dictionary defines as "a sum of money set aside for a particular purpose," also known as a *budget*.

A budget is a plan of your future income and expenses that you can use as a guideline for spending and saving. Money in and money out. You've probably heard, "Just spend less than you make and you'll be okay."

Budgeting isn't new. The concept is simple; however, simple doesn't mean easy.

Creating a budget is a critical step for every wealth building journey. There are three phases to building financial wealth. The first phase is to have a balanced or break-even budget, where our expenses and income are equal. Second, save money and build an emergency fund. We'll discuss the third phase, investing in a separate chapter.

How do you feel when you hear the word *budget*? What are the first thoughts and pictures that pop onto your head when you think about the work that goes into formulating a budget? The words and methods we use to describe the action don't matter nearly as much as our attitude about the activity.

Maybe you've tried unsuccessfully to reach personal finance goals in the past. If you've been frustrated or discouraged trying to manage your money, you're not alone. Take a few moments and consider your thoughts and feelings about the idea.

Getting to a point where more money is consistently coming into your bank account than going out can be difficult. Too many people take on high interest debt, which prevents wealth accumulation. Data shows more than half of Americans carry a credit card balance from month to month. Gen X-ers are the most anxious about it, with half saying their credit card debt is moderately or extremely stressful. Through the COVID pandemic, Americans took on more credit card debt, and any continue to use credit cards to cover essential living expenses. This is more common among younger generations: 61% of Gen Z-ers and 53% of millennials use credit cards for living expenses.[94]

If you find the topic or prospect of sticking to a financial plan daunting, consider finding a coach. Much like an athletic or fitness coach helps individuals set and reach health goals, a financial coach can help you work through challenges and guide you to achieve financial milestones.

There's a difference between coaching and advising. Yes, costs range and can run into the hundreds of dollars per hour. Don't let cost become an excuse for not consulting a financial coach. You can find well-qualified financial coaches for free.

The federal government's Internal Revenue Service (IRS) helps to operate and certify local Volunteer Income Tax Assistance (VITA) and Tax Counseling for the Elderly (TCE) programs. As you would guess, the primary focus is to provide free basic tax return preparation to qualified individuals. These nationwide programs have been operating for over fifty years. You can have your taxes prepared for free if you

- Earn $57,000 or less, or
- Are a person with a disability, or
- Have limited fluency in English.

Those sixty years of age and older can get free tax help through the TCE program. The sites specialize in questions about pensions and retirement-related issues unique to seniors.

Well-established community organizations that provide many other services run the sites.[95] In Boston, I helped create free financial fitness checkups at VITA sites citywide. The program has grown to serve many thousands of people and has developed lofty goals such as improving the credit score for every Boston resident through a United Way–supported program called Boston Builds Credit.[96]

## We All Face Difficulties

Why should you budget? To put it simply, life happens. Life happens to all of us, and it rarely goes according to our plan. In fact, as I write this, the world is continuing to deal with a pandemic. COVID-19 has changed the trajectory of nations and has disrupted the lives of people across the planet. Budgeting is an area where financial psychology and the nuts and bolts knowledge overlap.

Personally, the past few years have been challenging. Just before the pandemic, doctors diagnosed me with cholangiocarcinoma, bile duct cancer. This rare and aggressive disease ravaged my body. Doctors diagnosed my father-in-law with lung cancer six months after my diagnosis. Since my in-laws live with us, I became both a caregiver and a patient. My wife had to care for all of us, which was a monumental task. At times, I was too sick to drive, cook, or perform other basic daily tasks.

We're grateful for the lifesaving skills of the medical staff, who selflessly put their lives on the line during the COVID-19 pandemic. We're grateful for the health insurance that has helped us pay for the many surgeries, medications, and appointments with many specialists. I am grateful for the lifesaving gift of a liver transplant.

I'm not in search of sympathy; rather, I offer my experience as an example of life circumstances that millions of people every year have to deal with. Unexpected health challenges will come. Job loss will come. Car, home, or other large repair expenses will come. It's not a matter of if, but when. Since we can't avoid the unexpected but inevitable twists and turns of life, the best we can do is to plan, prepare, and remain flexible. It's more than okay for plans to change; adaptability is necessary for survival.

Life happens to all of us, often in the most unexpected ways and at unexpected times. I was, for all intents and purposes, a healthy young man. Cancer changed our finances.

There was the cost of copays, frequent hospital travel, and other incidental expenses, which were all necessary but unexpected. Illness significantly affected my income because on many days, my biggest accomplishment was just to sit up and survive.

Without planning, we will be at the whim of someone else's ideas. We become a rudderless ship, a directionless vessel. If, however, we hold on to our rudder firmly and faithfully steer with great intent, we can block and tackle through the adventurous journey and accomplish unimaginable victories.

## Living Paycheck-to-Paycheck

You may find yourself among the 38 million US households who spend everything earned in a given pay period. This is also called living paycheck-to-paycheck. Over two-thirds of those households are not poor, according to the National Bureau of Economic Research (NBER).[97]

In a research paper titled "The Wealthy Hand-to-Mouth," NBER authors found that both the wealthy who were living paycheck-to-paycheck, those with little or no liquid wealth, and the poor people living paycheck-to-paycheck behave similarly: both groups spend money as quickly as they get cash into their hands.

While the poor households are most frequently young people with low incomes, the wealthy people in the study are older, have high incomes, and hold substantial illiquid assets like stocks, which take time to access.[98]

Many of the clients I've counseled live in the suburbs of Boston, a relatively wealthy area—some of the most expensive places in the US to live. I've spoken with families who have a $1,200 monthly car payment, yet struggle to buy groceries. Others have grand multimillion-dollar homes, yet can't afford to furnish them, since they live paycheck-to-paycheck. The urge and social pressure to "keep up with the Joneses" is significant. Just because someone looks successful doesn't mean they have their financial act together.

It's far less stressful to look poor and be rich. In fact, in the book *The Millionaire Next Door*, authors Thomas J. Stanley and William D. Danko describe the cars (think Ford not Bugatti) and clothes (75% never paid more than $199 for shoes) the average millionaire owns. This interesting book breaks stereotypes that wealthy people have fancy cars and expensive stuff. The authors state that millionaires "believe that financial independence is more important than displaying high social status."[99]

You might ask, "What's all this got to do with me?" Millions of people spend money as soon as they get it. It is possible that you are in a situation where your current income doesn't cover your expenses. Well, the beauty of a spending plan is that it's simple. The challenge, again, is that simple doesn't mean easy.

If you're falling short of your personal money goals or you're running a deficit, meaning you're spending more than you earn, there are two variables to focus on. You can (1) increase your income, or (2) reduce your spending. Like many things in life, this can be much easier to say than to do.

I've had the privilege of learning through facilitating hundreds of group discussions about managing money. Many tips about reducing spending that I share are the collective wisdom of those who have done so. Some of the most expert budgeters I've met have been people in dire straits.

One group of men in rural New Hampshire were fighting for custody of their children when the mothers were unsafe. The participants of the group worked with a local social service agency to help with advocacy, since they all lacked the means to hire a lawyer. On one particular day, a gentleman shared how he saved on his grocery bill by "growing his own meat." He got a piglet for free from a local farmer. He fed the pig by getting vegetables and fruits past their prime for free from local farmers. At the time of the class, the pig weighed about 250 pounds. That's a lot of free meat.

I'm not suggesting that you run out and start a backyard farm with chickens and hogs. I tell this story as an example to help you think out of the box. When that father shared about his farming experience, sparks of creativity went through the room filled with other men in similar circumstances with similar opportunities. None of the other participants had thought of the idea before. You might not start raising animals, but maybe you can start a garden or find *ugly,* less-than-perfect produce at discount prices. We all need food to survive. You can talk to your neighbors or others around you to get ideas that will help you reach your goals.

I've led other groups where we share different recipes for common inexpensive ingredients such as beans. The cookbook *Good and Cheap* by Leanne Brown might be a helpful resource for you to learn to feed yourself on a $4-a-day food stamp budget (the ebook download is free): https://www.leannebrown .com/cookbooks/.[100]

Your budget may just need minor tweaks. Try going meatless one day per week to reduce the expense of meat. Reduce or eliminate eating out or taking family vacations. There's not a right or wrong way here. Work toward the goal of aligning your spending with your personal values.

Sometimes, a few alterations still won't get you to a balanced budget. On more than one occasion, I've had a conversation where significant changes were necessary to make the household budget ends meet. It's heartbreaking to discuss selling a family home because it's not affordable.

I remember one particular conversation with Sharon, a mother of three, who was living in her childhood home. Her husband had a significant reduction in income because of health challenges, and the family didn't have the possibility of increasing their household income. The principal and interest payment on their mortgage accounted for over 80% of the family's income. Sharon and her husband simply couldn't afford to make the mortgage payments and still pay for other necessities like taxes, utilities, and food. Not to mention ongoing home maintenance, transportation, clothes for growing children—you get the point.

To Sharon, the home represented so much more than a mortgage payment. Sharon and her family made memories in the place. It represented the possibility of passing on a family treasure to a future generation. The inability to pay the mortgage brought feelings of failure and despair. It devastated her.

## Keep It Personal

Have you tried to budget and failed? It is a frustrating and discouraging feeling. One method might work for someone you know, but that doesn't automatically mean that it's the best for you. Any system may work for the short term, but we're in this for the long haul and on the path to financial well-being. Figure out what will assist you in reducing stress, while maintaining accuracy. Just as it would be incredibly frustrating to dig a fifty-foot trench with a screwdriver, it's useful to find the right financial tool for the job.

Determining the best system for you is a personal decision based on personality and level of comfort with technology, among other factors. In our household, my wife and I use a spreadsheet to track our income and expenses. Due to pay schedules, a monthly budget works for us. Horizontally at the top, we have each month listed. Vertically, on the left side of the worksheet, we list each expense or category of expenses. Every dollar we spend falls into a unique category. For instance, we separate $100 spent at the grocery store into different categories on our spreadsheet. Some of the money is for household items like cleaning supplies, while we spend another amount on food.

Some expenses are fixed (the same every month), such as our internet bill, while other expenses are variable depending on our usage, such as gas for the cars. A budget is fluid and dynamic. During the COVID-19 pandemic, our consumption of gas for our cars has been minimal, but our cost of electricity has increased since we've been stuck in the house much more than ever before.

Let's not neglect periodic expenses. Subscriptions, annual memberships, vehicle maintenance, home repairs, and back-to-school clothes and supplies are a few examples. In our house, we estimate our monthly expenses by taking the previous year's data and dividing the average annual expenses by twelve to have an accurate monthly budgeted amount.

We heat our home with oil. Since we live in New England, heat is necessary but can be difficult to budget for because the monthly cost of the heating oil varies wildly throughout the year. We purchase our oil by the tank. During the winter months, our cost for oil is really high because we use a lot, but after about April or May, one tank will carry us through until October or so. We make sure we're saving money through the summer months to pay for heat during the inevitable winter. Many utility companies will arrange a monthly payment plan to even out the cost of home heating.

Cars are expensive. Remote working and programs like rideshare/car share may make vehicle ownership unnecessary. Calculate the costs of all options, determine the worth of lifestyle quality/convenience, and determine what's best for your situation.

Let's not forget the ongoing costs of car ownership, including registration, taxes, insurance, license renewal, and routine maintenance. If you have a vehicle, you know that brakes, tires, windshield wipers, fluids, batteries, and too many more parts to mention will wear out.

You might hate spreadsheets and that's okay. Try something different. I've worked with many clients who use a cash-stuffing system. This method is also called the envelope system. The strategy uses a separate envelope for each category of spending and requires putting cash into each envelope as budgeted for groceries, utilities, and other expenses. For some households, this system relieves the stress of tracking every single expense to the penny. There's also something very real about using cash. Once an individual envelope is empty, that's it for the month. It can make strategies like Pay Yourself First (PYF) easier.

If you're not comfortable keeping envelopes of money around, a similar way of managing household finances would be to use multiple savings accounts.

You can even automate some of the budgeting process using direct deposit. If your primary income is from an employer, you may direct a predetermined amount of money into separate specified accounts. Check with your human resources department and your financial institution. You could have funds for your rent or mortgage payment and household expenses deposited into one account, and a separate account for food and groceries.

Treat your savings like a necessary bill. Emergencies aren't an if-they-happen event, but a when-they-happen situation. One rule of thumb is to work toward saving 10% of your income for unexpected expenses. The total amount saved depends on your personal tolerance for risk and the amount and likelihood your income will vary. If your income is primarily gig-based or from freelancing, you might go periods of time without income.

A rule of thumb is a guideline that works for many, but not all people. Spending less than 35% of your take home (net) income on housing expenses, 20% on transportation, 20% on other living expenses like food and clothes, and less than 5% on debt payments like credit card and student loan payments are guidelines that can be helpful if spending has been out of control. A different budgeting ratio is the 80/20 plan, 20% for savings and 80% for everything else. If you live by a Financial Independence, Retire Early (FIRE) budget, you might save and invest 70% or more of your income. We'll talk more about investing later. Rules of thumb can be useful. Just remember to keep budgeting personal.

Financial technology, or fintech, is an enormous industry. Like any technology-based product, it's only good if it's useful to you. There will always be the next great thing. I'm often asked about the best budgeting app. I encourage people to explore. Some people successfully use Mint for budgeting It is the #1 most downloaded personal finance app.[101] Others find something different they like in the Apple or Google Play store. Some programs are free, while others come at a cost. Some are simple, while others can provide powerful accounting. Remember, the key is to determine what works for you for the long term.

I've had other clients use low-tech, inexpensive tools like a large desk calendar or dry-erase board to keep track of their income and expenses.

The clients all had the goal of debt reduction/elimination. They wrote payment due dates on the calendar to ensure their payments were never late. We worked together to determine the monthly amount each could afford to make sure the balances owed were actually decreasing. Minimum payments barely cover the interest, and it takes many, many years to pay the amount owed. And paying that compound interest is brutal.

The key when determining the best system for tracking and controlling expenses is to choose strategies and tools that are right for you. Make sure your system is easy to maintain and tailored for you and your family. Get your family involved when you can. If they understand the budget, staying within the budget could be easier. It's also a timely opportunity to teach kids about personal finance. Communication with the other people in your household is key.

Dealing with money can be stressful. Maintaining a plan should reduce stress and frustration. A list of financial priorities will help you manage the money that you have. Think of the process as an ongoing habit that's built and refined with trial and error, not a one-time activity. Most systems can track expenses over a one-week or a one-month period. We're building wealth, and that takes consistency.

## Where's the Money?

You might be in a position where you're spending more every month than you're earning. The expense-reducing ability of families with the least amount of income has impressed me many times. It has humbled me on more than one occasion while speaking with homeless families and individuals living in emergency and family shelters. But there are certainly instances where expenses really can't reduce any further, and it's necessary to increase income.

Consider the many resources about side hustles. Begin by thinking about the skills you have and work from there. If you don't have skills that are in demand, invest in yourself and go learn them. I love the example from one inspiring entrepreneur I met in a homeless shelter. Kim lived in a family shelter, so she had access to a shared kitchen. She made mouth-watering empanadas and sold them to anyone and everyone. I invested in the business by buying plenty of the tasty treats. We explored bringing her business "legit" and found resources to help.[102]

If you're employed but underpaid, ask yourself why. What can change? Maybe your boss doesn't understand the value you bring to the company. Workplace discrimination is a possibility. Once you determine why you're underpaid, create an action plan. If prejudice is the cause, you might file a formal complaint, or even finding a lawyer. Your company is unlikely to volunteer to offer you more pay. Don't just ask for a raise; prove your worth. The president of the counseling agency I worked for explained why the top-earning employee made significantly more than others. The employee never took no for an answer when negotiating salary.

Should We Save Now or Later?

For some people, $1 per week is hard to save. That's fine. Don't compare yourself to people who may save and invest $100, $1,000, or more, per month. Save as much as you can, based on your personal circumstances. Keep moving toward your goal. As you work toward financial goals, you'll develop better money management habits. Financial discipline will serve you well at any income level.

To reduce the shock of unexpected expenses, financial advisers recommend saving 10% of your income until there's at least three and up to twelve or more months of living expenses set aside in a liquid account. Liquid means that you can access the money immediately, as with savings or money market accounts.

A three- to twelve-month savings cushion may feel impossible. If you're not stressed, it's likely someone very close to you is and could use your encouragement. The only way to tackle a monumental goal is by taking one small step at a time. Once you have a budget, you can identify how much you can dedicate to your individual financial goals. If you have debt, it's important to include repayment in your financial plan. Having an emergency savings account is essential, since unexpected expenses are inevitable.

My advice is to consider your individual risk tolerance, obligations, life circumstances, and the stability of your income to determine the balance of debt repayment and saving. For instance, if you have five kids, low risk tolerance, and an unreliable household income, you would do well to be conservative and work toward a larger-than-average emergency fund.

Your needs are different if you're single and healthy and you have a high risk tolerance and few expenses. You might not need as much for emergencies, but you may benefit from budgeting money to pay debts or invest aggressively.

## All about the Execution

You might budget to pay for unexpected medical bills, education, building emergency savings, or even buying a house. Once we work out our financial objectives, one significant challenge is to have the self-control to implement them. I find discipline challenging. My wife is a natural. She's an all-around rock star, an amazing person. In our house, she has far more discipline than I do. We've talked about this and we use our various strengths to optimize the well-being in our home. This is an important point in any relationship.

No one is great at everything. Take inventory of your natural strengths and weaknesses and develop systems and use tools that suit you. Make sure to keep the "personal" in personal finance.

I consider part of my wife's financial system antiquated. She maintains control of bill-paying by writing checks, placing them in a stamped envelope, and mailing them. You might say, "But it costs less to use electronic bill pay and you can track your payment." Well, do what works for you, and be consistent. She is incredible and her system works *for us*. Set your behaviors based on personal values and build your financial well-being by maintaining control through this developed order. Discipline is necessary for our goals to lead to accomplishment.

Budgeting, money management, asset allocation, resource strategy, fiscal estimate—whatever you call it—when you're disciplined and follow your personal plan, you will accomplish your goals. Even when the current is against you, "Just . . . keep . . . swimming." It can feel challenging to keep our heads above water. Don't give up.

While you're on your financial education journey, realize that you are part of a community. As you swim, look around once in a while. Others are feeling some of the same things you are. At one time, others swam where you are now and they can help guide you to safe harbors and assist you in reaching your potential. You are not alone.

Just keep swimming, or should I say just keep budgeting.

At its most basic, a spending plan includes income and expenses. In my experience, most people are unaware of how much they spend. I encourage you to:

- Keep track of every expense, and

- Make sure your records are accurate and detailed.

It's so easy to spend a couple dollars here and there, and as you probably understand, spending adds up quickly. All the little expenses add up quickly and can leave us wondering where our money went.

Sometimes the act of tracking expenses provides peace of mind. For some people, the practice may seem impossible. You may have a limited income and can't afford all of your essential bills each month. Creating a budget will help you prioritize expenses and better understand what's possible. Maybe you have more than enough income to pay your basic expenses, but fall short of reaching certain goals. Either way, working with the facts is essential. Gather your records and receipts and learn the best tracking tools and methods for you and your family.

By tracking your expenses, you'll have an accurate account of where your money is going. This exercise will increase your awareness and help you develop healthy habits. Mindfulness is a vital step in taking control of your money. If we're not in control, money will control us, and that can get ugly quickly. Excessive debt and stress are only two likely outcomes.

## More Than Dollars-and-Cents Decisions

As discussed earlier in this book, there are significant emotional aspects to dealing with money. As humans, we don't operate like *homo economicus*, the theoretical person who always makes rational self-interested choices and who pursues their goals in the most optimal way possible.

We are *homo sapiens*, human beings. We feel. Making family decisions often includes much more consideration than the dollars and cents of the circumstances. This is where having trusted and competent advisers comes in. Our friends and family can be helpful, *when they have proper knowledge and experience.* The right people can help in managing emotions and money.

When we seek advice, it's important the people that we speak with have expertise in the particular area we need help in. I wouldn't ask a chef how to complete a masonry project, and I might not get the best recipes from a bricklayer. Then again, the culinary expert and the mason may have well-established side hustles. Seek advice from someone with expertise in the area you need help with.

I remember some advice I received as a teenager. A friend told me that if you never file a tax return, then you never have to pay taxes. That sounded like brilliant advice to me! After all, I had cooler stuff to buy than to "waste" my money on taxes. To be clear, this is the perspective of a young teenager. As an adult, I fully endorse paying taxes. We need public schools, first responders, and things such as paved roads that our taxes pay for.

In the end, the only person who really lost out with that terrible advice was me. As a student making very little money, I would have received a refund of taxes my employer had withheld from my pay. The money I was greedily trying to hold on to ended up as a gift to Uncle Sam. The joke was on me.

You can find countless books on managing expenses. This chapter is not exhaustive, and that's intentional. We all understand the importance of spending less than we make. We've heard it a million times. It's pretty easy to "budget in a bubble," or implement a plan when everything in life works out perfectly with no hiccups. The real challenge is to maintain course when we get blindsided by life. It happens to the best of us.

## Persistence Goes a Long Way

Many of the most successful people didn't get to their positions from sheer talent. Michael Jordan, one of the most successful basketball players of all time, famously said, "I've missed more than 9,000 shots in my career. I've lost almost 300 games. Twenty-six times, I've been trusted to take the game-winning shot and missed. I've failed over and over and over again in my life. And that is why I succeed."[103]

Never . . . give . . . up.

As a high school dropout lacking marketable skills, I struggled to earn a living wage. I rode a bike to work and slept on a floor. I couldn't reduce my expenses much further. With each opportunity, my goal was to outwork my coworkers. Selling furniture in retail, I realized sales were more important than degrees. As a nineteen-year-old, I outsold all but one person at the Bombay Company where I worked. I was hungry and needed to eat. There were barriers and it was far from easy. I had a criminal record from my drug-dealing days. Few companies wanted to hire me, but once I built a solid employment record, the next job opportunity came easier.

When I started my first job in an office, I was out of place. This was in 1999 and the early 2000s. The first time I tried to send a fax for a customer, I accidentally sent it from one fax machine in the office to another across the room. I even needed help to send my first email.

While trying to stand out for my hustle, I eagerly sought opportunities to go above and beyond. So, when I saw a need to change the office's five-gallon water tank, I hoisted the fresh one onto my shoulder and moved to place it in the dispenser. Not knowing exactly how to do this, I dropped the bottle. It cracked. Exploded. Water splashed everywhere. As embarrassing as the event was, I never gave up. I studied diligently to increase my knowledge of the business and looked for ways to be extra-helpful. My pay increased over time because I added value to the company.

Be careful of the spending trap. I, like many people, spent more when I earned more. In a world where rampant consumerism drives us, it's tempting to display an image of wealth. One manager of a sales team I worked with encouraged all of his employees to have a vice. He understood that if it compelled his employees to spend—even spend more than they could comfortably afford—they would be driven to work harder to earn money to feed their compulsions.

When we manage our careers and finances by emotion, we're more likely to be dissatisfied and broke. Broke emotionally, spiritually, physically, and financially.

Sometimes the measures we take to make ends meet need to be significant. Opportunities might have to be found by moving to an unfamiliar area. You may find some places are too expensive to live comfortably in. Sharon and the family I mentioned earlier had to make the painful decision to move. The choice was more than just a line item on a budget; selling the family home was heart-wrenching. The solid middle-class couple faced circumstances beyond their control. We created a solution, but for Sharon, the experience was emotionally draining.

Most people can budget in a bubble with ideal circumstances. We can accomplish all kinds of amazing things when there are no distractions, challenges, worries, frustrations, bills, health problems, or competing demands or responsibilities.

Daily chaos makes it much more difficult to concentrate on the essential tasks required in everyday life. Writing this paragraph took two days. There were several interruptions from a demanding puppy, a son who likes to play with the puppy, and a snowstorm that required attention. It was challenging to focus and write a few sentences.

When we're stressed out, it's difficult to perform any activities, never mind budgeting. Determining our expenses and subtracting them from our income is far more complex than simple math, and distractions make the activity challenging. It's an emotional process. More than numbers, our budget reflects our priorities, hopes, and dreams.

# MONEY TALK Q&A

## Q: What is the best money management system?

A: The one that works for you and your family. By working, I mean sticking to the method for the long term. My wife and I have used Excel spreadsheets to keep track of our income and expenses. Some find mobile apps beneficial. The only way to know if they'll work for you is to try.

I worked with clients who like the Mint app (https://mint.intuit.com/); others like to use paper and pencil. I've spoken with many people who use the envelope method. They designate a separate envelope or container for each category of spending and calculate how much of their income needs to be "deposited" into each one. Some people take the same idea and open separate deposit accounts for each category.

Many financial institutions can work with your employer to separate the direct deposit of your payroll funds into multiple accounts. A budget has tremendous potential to save time and reduce stress.

If you'd like help with budgeting, consider the following resources:

- Federal Trade Commission (https://www.consumer .gov/articles/1002-making-budget)

- National Foundation for Credit Counseling (https://www.nfcc.org/)

## Q: I've tried budgeting systems and have a difficult time sticking to them. How can I develop better habits?

A: It takes time for new behaviors to become automatic. I've found that a partner who will motivate, encourage, and hold me accountable is invaluable. The *New York Times* bestselling author James Clear has some proven strategies in his book, *Atomic Habits: An Easy & Proven Way to Build Good Habits & Break Bad Ones.*

## Q: How can I compare the cost of living in different areas?

A: EPI's family budgets (https://www.epi.org/resources/budget/) provide a more accurate and complete measure of economic security in America.

## Q: Where can I go for career resources?

A: ONET Online, www.onetonline.org, and Career One Stop, www.careeronestop.org, are resources to identify career growth opportunities. There are also plenty of resources for you to start or grow a business:

- America's SBDC (https://americassbdc.org/) is one place where you can get connected to local free business consulting.

- SCORE (www.score.org/) offers access to free workshops, advice from experienced mentors, and a Small Business Resource Library.

## Q: What if I can't pay a student loan?

A: Take action as soon as possible. You may qualify for for-bearance, loan forgiveness, or other relief. Check out Federal Student Aid (https://studentaid.gov/).

## Q: Where can I go for tax help?

A: Start here at the websites of the IRS and government benefits:

- www.irs.gov/help/ita
- www.benefits.gov/benefit/1543

If you'd like to find your nearest VITA site, free worksheets, and a family budget calculator that will help identify living wages and economic security in America, visit www.MattParadise.com/capablebonus.

# 12

## STOP DEFERRING DREAMS

### Set Goals

What are your desires and ambitions? We all have different values and aspirations. They're essential. From scientific advancement to artistic masterpieces to radical social change, many historic accomplishments came about through longing for improvement. As the poet Langston Hughes said, "Hold fast to dreams, for if dreams die, life is a broken-winged bird that cannot fly."[104]

To achieve success, we must move beyond desires or momentary intentions. Goal setting helps guide us toward success and keeps us motivated. Accomplishing goals requires deliberate action. Reaching goals often involves as much mental energy as it does physical energy.

Dream. Dream big, bold audacious dreams. Hold tight to them. Imagine them as vividly as if you could actually touch them. Once they're clear in your mind, take one step toward them. No matter how big or small that step might be. And then take another step. And another. Before you know it, you'll be well on your way.

When I was twenty-five, my wife and I bought our first house. We were renting a nice enough apartment, but we desired to build a bigger life. We wanted to have at least one child, host friends and family, establish long-term roots in a neighborhood, and contribute to a community we could call home.

To start out, we created a vision board of sorts. It wasn't a collage or cute artwork, but pictures from our research. For weekend dates, we explored lots of open houses together. We imagined living in specific neighborhoods. We touched the front doors, smelled the air, and heard location-specific sounds. All of this motivated us toward our goal.

Once we planned to purchase, we began aggressively saving every penny we could for a down payment. We didn't eat out or spend money going out for coffee or buy extra stuff we didn't really need. We created a budget that included paying for necessities and saving money for our target. It was exciting to move closer and closer to our goal.

The house we finally purchased was a home we could picture living in for the rest of our lives. It was the smallest home in the nicest neighborhood we could afford. There was significant buildable land, which was useful for our plans.

One year after our purchase, we built an addition for my wife's aging parents, who were retired and considering their options. We considered nursing homes brutal and decided that, if possible, we would avoid that choice. As the oldest sister without brothers, my wife bore the cultural expectation of caring for her parents.

We hired an architect to design the dream apartment for my in-laws. The combined living arrangement has allowed us to care for them through retirement and health challenges. Though it hasn't always been easy, the decision has enriched our lives.

Homeownership isn't for everyone. A home is often more expensive than people realize. We began by considering the math. After running the numbers, we determined that if we invested the difference between our rent and the cost of home-ownership, we would have ended up ahead by investing. If our focus had been purely financial, we would have made other choices. Multigenerational living isn't for everyone, either. The financial and emotional decisions are complex.

## Your Wealthy Life Is Different from Mine. And That's Okay.

We must each ask ourselves, "What kind of life do I want to live?"

Here are a few simple questions that may require some deep introspection:

- How do you define wealth?
- How do you define success?
- What do you want from life?

What steps are you taking toward your objectives? Your path to well-being is very much an emotional, psychological, and mental journey. We're human and our thoughts, attitudes, behaviors, and emotions are complex. No one can tell you that your personal value system is right or wrong.

Many advertisers and marketers work to influence our values and tug at our heartstrings. They make every effort to manipulate us as consumers. They rely on themes like thrift and best value, family, personal fulfillment, inspiration, health, and love. Consumers often purchase products and services when the corporate philosophy *seems* to align with personal and/or family values. That's marketing.

We must be in control of our money rather than let our money and marketing control us. A house full of stuff and a heart devoid of joy makes for a life of misery. When our values are clearly defined, we can take control of our daily decisions and work toward our goals with intention.

In "An Interview with God," author and humanitarian Jim Brown wrote:

> "What surprises you most about humankind?"
>
> "Many things.
>
> "That they get bored of being children, are in a rush to grow up, and then long to be children again. That they lose their health to make money and then lose their money to restore health. That by thinking anxiously about the future, they forget the present, and live neither for the present nor for the future. That they live as if they will never die, and die as if they had never lived."[105]

What do you consider a good life or a life well lived?

You may ask, "How do I align my personal values with my personal/family goals?" I've found that this is easier said than done. It certainly takes concerted effort and deliberate planning.

I have encountered many clients whose personal values don't match their day-to-day life choices, resulting in discontented lives. This chapter isn't about minimizing challenges. We all face difficult circumstances. Perspective makes all the difference.

I had difficulty recovering from my cancer treatments and liver transplant. It hurt for me to breathe and it was painful for me to sit, but movement aids recovery. It confronted me with a choice. The urge to relax and enjoy moments of pain-medicated comfort was enticing, but I moved. Every step was excruciating. But I wanted to be well.

My focus moved from the pain to the goal I was striving for. Tears of gratitude roll down my cheeks when I think of the hospital staff and other patients encouraging me toward my goal of recovering my health.

## What's Holding You Back?

We've covered personal values. Now let's talk about goals, barriers, and working toward well-being. Anyone who has set a resolution knows how difficult it is to reach the goal. Consider these statistics:

- Research shows that 50% of adults make New Year's resolutions, but fewer than 10% keep them for more than a few months.

- People often give up on New Year's resolutions due to difficulty breaking old habits, focusing on specific outcomes, or they have a weak emotional connection to the goal.

- You can increase your chances of achieving your New Year's resolutions by setting realistic and achievable process goals that will help you form new habits, as well as following other steps for success.[106]

Sticking to goal setting is challenging. To overcome inertia or lack of motivation, some people use commitment devices to avoid procrastination by committing to a goal. Commitment devices have two major features: they're voluntarily adopted and implemented, and they tie consequences to follow-through failures.

For instance, after you create a detailed goal, you can have an accountability partner to help accomplish it. To have a commitment device in place, you can write a check to a charity that you really don't care to support. Maybe you're not a pet person and you write a check to the local animal shelter. The amount should be enough that it would be a sacrifice, but not so much that it would jeopardize meeting your financial obligations. You would then give the check (or cash) to your friend and tell them to send the money if you don't reach your stated goal. This would give you significant motivation (and worst case, you could help some cute puppies).

The commitment device doesn't have to be money. It could be an athletic challenge, or service challenge, such as cleaning up trash or anything that provides motivation. Ultimately, do what works for you. I've found that having an accountability partner is really helpful. Having someone who can cheer us on and provide coaching along the way can increase our chances of success.

Keep your vision in clear focus and do what it takes to stay motivated. Think about it. Talk about it. Work toward it, and as you do, your actions will become habits.

When creating a goal, many find the SMART goal framework helpful. The acronym stands for

- **S**pecific: Make your goals detailed. (What? Why? How?)

- **Me**asurable: Be precise. Rather than saving "some money," use an exact dollar amount. (How much?)

- **A**chievable: Is reaching this goal possible with effort and commitment? (What steps are involved?)

- **R**ealistic (also Review and Revise): What skills, knowledge, and resources are necessary to reach the goal? Some goals are achievable, but may take more time, effort, or money than you're willing to spend. It's also important to review goals and revise as necessary. If you fall short on reaching a goal, don't give up. The time frame may need to be adjusted. Celebrate the fact that you made progress and continue on.

- **T**ime-bound: When will you achieve this goal? If you are a procrastinator, this is a critical component of goal setting. Many people have a dream of retiring "someday" but lack a plan to make it happen.

As you work toward your goals, it's helpful to remember why you're doing it. Are you saving for a child's education? Your family might be your why. Are you working, saving, and investing so that you can stop trading time for money? Financial freedom might be your why. We're more likely to stay motivated and reach goals when we remember why we work so hard.

Because life happens to us all, think through any potential obstacles and solutions for your plans. For instance, I overthink and procrastinate. Keeping this in mind, when I set out to write this book, I told many friends and family members my intent. This motivated me to get the writing done. Another common obstacle is trying to be perfect and/or fearing failure. I realized that if I waited until this book was perfect in every way, it wouldn't be completed, never mind published. The project came to fruition because of the help of outstanding editors, book designer, and early draft readers who provided feedback and encouragement. The idea of "self-made" is a fallacy. Always keep in mind, appreciate, and acknowledge the people who help you.

It's so easy to be consumed by everyday life and neglect strategic planning. Life happens to everybody. Financial well-being and life are about the journey, not just a focus on the destination. Goals aren't set in stone. When the unexpected happens, extend grace (lots of grace) and remain calm.

The statistics about how people give up on their resolutions have been about the same for decades. I don't believe that most people give up because of a lack of motivation. It's really, really difficult to persevere through the challenges, adversity, and day-to-day demands of our lives.

Sometimes it's impossible to follow through with plans once the chaos comes. The diagnosis of bile duct cancer upended our lives. Our goals and plans were all but abandoned. Day-to-day was a matter of survival, and it wasn't clear that I'd live. Gratefully, I received a life-changing liver transplant and now have the chance to see our son grow up.

Some of our goals needed a readjustment. No matter how tough life may be, we don't have to abandon our dreams and goals; however, we may need to revise them from time to time. For you, it may mean that an accomplishment will take three years instead of one. That's okay. It's about the direction we're moving. We're moving toward the goal or away from it, and our direction determines the outcome.

Sometimes it feels like we're taking one step forward and two steps back. Other times, we might review our goals and realize that our values and/or priorities have changed. Creating a values-based plan with goals is helpful for items both big and small. Just because something is a short-term goal, or a less-expensive goal, doesn't make it less important. You might save for dinner and a movie. No goal is too small. No judgment. Go for it.

Whether or not you choose the structure of SMART goals, it's helpful to separate goals into three different time frames and then prioritize them.

- Short-term: Three months

- Medium-term: Three months to a year

- Long-range: More than one year

First, think about short-term goals—those you can reach in about three months. These might include saving enough money for the children's holiday presents, taking yourself to the beach for a day, or buying a new big-screen television for your home.

Set medium-term goals that can be reached in three months to about a year. These might include trading in your car for the pickup truck you've always wanted, learning to sew your own clothes, or signing up for a class at your local community college.

Finally, think about long-range goals that are more than a year away. Perhaps you've always wanted to go back to school for a degree or certification, start or expand your business, or buy a home.

When you assign a priority rank for each goal, be sure to include the achievement date, the total cost, and the weekly cost for each goal. Most people find it more manageable to budget using weekly expenses. It's easy to be overwhelmed with large numbers. This is also one way to determine if your goal is realistic.

As you set and reach goals on the path toward financial well-being, take time to reflect on your successes. Celebrate even the smallest of accomplishments. When you fall short of a particular goal, learn from it and rejoice that you can keep going. If you never fall short of a goal, set the bar higher. And by all means necessary, stop comparing your accomplishments to what other people have attained.

Too often, I catch myself in this comparison trap. When I notice it, I stop, take a deep breath (or ten), and remember that my journey is different. We can learn lessons from each other; however, comparing others' successes and failures to ours will crush us.

Courageously take one step at a time. Include others on the journey. Don't stop when obstacles make the road rough. Remember that the difficulty and suffering we endure requires perseverance. Perseverance develops character and strength. Character leads to hope. And one day, we can stop asking, "What happens when dreams are deferred?"

# MONEY TALK Q&A

## Q: How can I help kids with their goals?

A: You can be an outstanding model. Demonstrate how you reach goals. Kids are terrific at learning through watching. Here are some helpful book suggestions:

- *Salt In His Shoes: Michael Jordan in Pursuit of a Dream* by Deloris Jordan, Roslyn M. Jordan, and Kadir Nelson

- *Growth Mindset Workbook for Kids: 55 Fun Activities to Think Creatively, Solve Problems, and Love Learning* by Peyton Curley

- *The Self-Driven Child: The Science and Sense of Giving Your Kids More Control Over Their Lives* by William Stixrud PhD and Ned Johnson

## Q: I've tried SMART goals, vision boards, and many other methods and still have trouble with setting and sticking to goals. What can I do?

A: There are many structures for the goal-setting process. Indeed has a list of ten techniques, and while they focus on career, the methods apply to any goal: https://www.indeed.com /career-advice/career-development/goal-setting-techniques.

I've found that reaching goals is less about the method we use; often, the challenge is emotional. We all encounter road-blocks on our growth journey.

Here are some books you may find helpful.

- *I Am That Girl: How to Speak Your Truth, Discover Your Purpose, and #bethatgirl* by Alexis Jones
- *Your Best Year Ever: A 5-Step Plan for Achieving Your Most Important Goals* by Michael Hyatt
- *The Desire Map: A Guide to Creating Goals with Soul* by Danielle LaPorte
- *The Power of Positive Thinking* by Norman Vincent Peale
- *Burnout: The Secret to Unlocking the Stress Cycle* by Emily Nagoski PhD and Amelia Nagoski DMA
- *The ONE Thing: The Surprisingly Simple Truth About Extraordinary Results* by Gary Keller and Jay Papasan
- *Why Has Nobody Told Me This Before?* by Dr. Julie Smith (you can find her life changing insights on TikTok @drjuliesmith)

For encouragement, inspiration, and a free SMART goals tool, visit www.MattParadise.com/capablebonus.

# 13

## GLOW UP

### Transitioning from Saving to Investing

Have you seen a child shop for toys? There are so many fun choices, and retailers know how to make every option irresistible. Children get excited and have a hard time controlling themselves. Joy, wonder, and awe are a few emotions that accompany wide smiles and gleaming eyes. Retailers create their environment with intention and craft the shopping experience to be enticing. Companies fight to gain additional customers and motivate employees to sell more. The same selling principals apply to online shopping and for products targeted toward all age groups.

There are an overwhelming number of wealth-building products, services, and strategies. It's confusing when every company and expert proclaims their way as the best way. Much of personal finance is simple. Don't confuse simple with easy.

We discussed the first two phases of wealth building: maintaining a balanced budget and building an emergency fund. In this chapter, we'll discuss the third phase of financial planning—building financial wealth through investing.

Quick question: Would you rather have $1 million today or a penny and double your money every day for a month? The million dollars sounds nice, doesn't it? What would you buy? A new car? A house?

If you chose the penny, you've either heard this before, or you know the power of compounding. If you start with a penny and double it every day, in a month, it compounds to $10.7 million! It starts off slowly, but with some time, the magic of math kicks in.

> Day 2: You would have $0.02
> Day 3: You would have $0.04
> Day 4: You would have $0.08
> Day 18: You would have $1,310.72
> Day 28: You would have $1,342,177.28
> Day 31: You would have $10,737,418.24

Wouldn't it be great if we could start with a penny and become multi-millionaires? It would be amazing if banks paid 100% daily interest on our savings. Let me ask another question. Would you like to double your money? Stick with me here. There is a simple calculation to figure out how it's possible.

People find the equation for calculating compound interest complicated. Few people use it and most people instead turn to calculators. Some have said that compound interest is the most powerful force in the world. Banks and businesses understand its power. If you understand it, you will earn it. If you don't understand it, you'll pay it to someone else.

The Rule of 72 makes compound interest easier to understand. If you'd like to double your money, pay attention to this one:

72/APR = Number of Years to Double Your Money

This is an important concept. Let's dig in a little more. As mentioned earlier, APR stands for annual percentage rate. This is used to calculate how much interest we pay when borrowing money. Yes, every time we use a credit card, we're borrowing from the bank. The Rule of 72 also applies to annual percentage yield (APY), which is the return on an investment. Let's consider the following example: If you invested or borrowed $500 with an interest rate of 10%, it would take just over seven years to double the amount to $1,000—72 divided by 10% APR equals about seven years.

Math is only one part of the wealth-building equation. It's also important to understand our own personalities, knowledge, and investing style. We must understand the environment—the markets in which we invest. Are you a rational investor who makes most decisions by the numbers? Or are you an idealist who has a tendency to care less about money than about other goals? Maybe you're a guardian and are cautious with money. You might be an artisan and lean toward the freewheeling and daring side.

Most people have a blend of personalities. I'm an idealist mixed with a rationalist personality. I really enjoy helping others even when it comes at a personal cost, but also require logic. Careless action that places my family in financial jeopardy hurts them and limits our ability to help others.

## Make Your Money Work

There is a difference between saving and investing. Saving money is necessary for living expenses and unexpected bills. Savings are helpful for your short- and mid-term goals and for getting through unforeseeable circumstances.

Investing is all about putting your money to work for you. It's never too soon to invest. Think about owning a piece of your favorite company. For my son, it's Roblox. Well, you can buy stock, which is a share in the business. When it does well, you can make money. If the company goes bankrupt, you could lose all of your money. It's really dangerous to invest money you can't afford to lose.

Following terrible advice from a coworker, friend, or even an unscrupulous financial adviser could leave you frustrated, unprepared, overwhelmed, or harmed. Many financial advisers provide standard advice that they consider applicable to all. Not all advisers are created equal, and many don't operate as fiduciaries. A fiduciary is someone who has a legal responsibility to provide financial advice that is in your best interest.

Several years ago, the credit counseling agency I worked for used a well-known investment firm for our retirement funds. I'll never forget my surprise when the 401(k) representative called me for advice and counseling. He had accumulated more than $75,000 in credit card debt with interest rates higher than 20%.

Salomon Smith Barney required him to use personal credit cards to charge various client expenses. The charges were from client retention and acquisition. It was a fake-it-till-you-make-it situation. Unfortunately, though the expenses were part of the job, they did not reimburse most. This so-called financial adviser was incentivized by Salomon Smith Barney to nudge our employees to invest in funds with higher fees. Can you see the conflict of interest? He was stuck in a difficult position. He was trying to make ends meet. Unfortunately, it came at a cost to his personal budget and the employees he was advising.

The fees charged by fund managers can significantly erode gains. This is part of the reason Warren Buffett, one of the most successful investors, recommends investing in *index funds* over the long term.[107] An *index fund* is typically a group of stocks and bonds that match the market's performance. One advantage they have is very low investment management fees. A second benefit is that they follow the broad market, rather than trying to pick individual stocks, which can be dangerous.

Maurie Backman, the Motley Fool author, wrote, "Back in 1999, a chimpanzee named Raven picked stocks by throwing darts at a board. Her portfolio ultimately outperformed over 6,000 money managers by scoring a whopping 213% return for the year. And years later, a Russian circus chimp named Lusha assembled a portfolio that beat 94% of Russia's mutual funds. Kind of makes you question the benefit of paying the experts." Backman's article reported a cat had better financial returns than its competition of "professionals."[108]

Now that's embarrassing. So it's not impossible to beat the stock market, but it's very unlikely. There is no shortage of get rich quick schemes. For building wealth through the stock market, consistency over the long term with reliable assets is the strategy most likely to benefit you.

Investing in *equities* is a popular way to build wealth, although it comes with risk. An equity investment is money that's invested in a company by purchasing shares of that company in the stock market. We typically trade these shares on a stock exchange. The higher the potential return on investment, the greater the possibility of losing money.

Many employees invest in their company's retirement fund and may not know they're investing in the stock market. This again highlights the idea that your 401(k), 403(b), or other sponsored retirement plan administrator likely isn't providing the education necessary to help you understand the basics—never mind enough information to become a competent investor.

Investment advice can be overwhelming. Don't stress over it. We can learn from mistakes, but worry, fear, and anxiety can lead to emotional and physical disease. Even if you get rich, you'll be unwell and lack whole health wealth. Getting appropriate advice is a wise practice. Before investing your hard-earned cash, learn about options and the pros and cons of each choice.

## What Is the Future of Investing?

Investments will continue to change and develop with technology, creativity, and regulation. The fundamental principles of personal finance are centuries old and will remain relevant.

Some businesses use tokenized equity. The term refers to digital tokens or "coins," which represent equity shares in a corporation or organization. Issuing shares as digital assets, such as crypto coins or tokens, can be a convenient way to raise capital for businesses. Investors may benefit from the potential of lower fees and greater control over investments.

Consider four primary goals when investing in equities:

1. **Growth**

2. **Income**

3. **Tax benefits**

4. **Hedge against inflation**

With stocks, *growth* means that the company has significant potential for capital appreciation. You've probably heard of capital gain, which is the profit you make when you sell an asset for more than you bought it for. Some people apply the concept to side hustles all the time. Platforms like Amazon and eBay are filled with sellers who walk into their local discount store, purchase items, and sell them for profit. Now imagine earning money just for owning the stuff.

Growth investing is different from value investing, where the price of the company's stock is trading below where it should be for reasons that are likely to change in the foreseeable future. I'd love to get a check for the junk in my garage. Not realistic, but owning certain stocks can be a significant source of income.

Buy low and sell high is the name of the game. Profits made from selling assets you've owned for a year or less are called short-term capital gains. Gains from assets owned for longer than a year are long-term capital gains.

Cash flow is another term for *income*. Real estate investing is one way to generate positive cash flow, but there are many more choices. You can buy ATMs or other money-generating assets like laundry mats, vending machines, and auto rentals. Each business has pros and cons, but real estate is a popular choice and has built many fortunes. We'll discuss this further in a moment.

They pay dividend income from the profits of a company to the stockholders. An example is Coca-Cola (NYSE: KO), which pays investors a reliable dividend that has yielded about 3% annually. This is higher than the average S&P 500 stock, which yields about 1.6%. I'm not suggesting Coca-Cola is the best for dividends, since there are other possibilities with higher yields and not much more risk.

So why would companies pay shareholders? Ultimately, companies have three options for their stocks when they make

Financially Capable

a profit. They can reinvest the earnings into the business, buy back stock, or pay dividends to shareholders. There are various reasons for each, but I'll stick to personal finance and not dive into corporate finance and strategy.

If you're fortunate to have money from capital gains, dividends, or other investments, then you'll have to consider a *tax strategy*. I say strategy since there are multiple tax rates and it's often worthwhile to consult with a tax professional as you continue to grow your wealth. People often pay the highest taxes on the money they earn from their jobs, while investment income is usually taxed at a lower rate.

The tax rate on qualified dividends can be 0%, 15%, or 20%, depending on your taxable income and filing status. The tax rate on nonqualified dividends is the same as the tax rate on your regular income tax bracket. In both cases, people in higher tax brackets pay a higher dividend tax rate. Qualified dividends are dividends from shares in domestic companies and certain qualified foreign companies that are held for at least a specific minimum period, known as the holding period.

We've discussed how inflation makes the stuff we buy more expensive. How can we protect or *hedge against inflation*? Real estate, savings bonds, stocks, precious metals like silver and gold, Treasury Inflation Protected Securities (TIPS), which are loans to the US Government, and cryptocurrency are all examples of assets that potentially combat the effects of inflation. Low-yield savings accounts, cash under a mattress, or money buried in the ground are examples that will lose purchasing power value with inflation.

High inflation can make it difficult for many people to cover basic expenses. In 2022, the inflation rate broke records as it rose above 9%. Higher prices for essential items, such as food, gasoline, and shelter, add to the burdens faced by many families. Inflation that's too low can weaken the economy. Low inflation usually means an environment of low interest rates. Low rates are good for borrowing, but not great for saving.

## Managing Risk for Success

President John Kennedy said, "There are risks and costs to action. But they are far less than the long range risks of comfortable inaction."[109]

There's a risk-reward correlation to investing. High investment risks have high potential returns. Low-risk investments will yield nothing to write home about. In fact, keeping all of your money in cash or its equivalent can be dangerous in the long run when you factor in inflation. This is not a suggestion to avoid saving. Remember phase 2, save money and build an emergency fund. Whole health wealth is about saving *and* investing.

If you're unsure about your personal investing risk tolerance, there is a link to a free assessment in the Money Talk Q&A section of this chapter. Uncertainty is part of life. It's risky to never invest.

When you're investing, first establish your vision for the future, then set a goal and determine the resources and tools that will best help you accomplish the stated goal. If your goal is to enjoy a long career and invest throughout your working life with the dream of retiring in the distant future, you might consider your employer's 401(k), 403(b), or similar work-based retirement plan. The accounts are tax-deferred and funded with pretax money. Contributions reduce your current taxable income and allow you to put money away for the future.

Don't get discouraged if it seems like everyone around you is a millionaire and feeling great about their wealth. They're not. Don't worry if you *feel* less successful than others. In fact, according to Fidelity Investments well-being research, more than half of American workers say they are "extremely or very concerned" about the health and stability of the economy.[110]

If your goal is to have a net worth above $1 million, go for it. There are millions of millionaires. With hard work, healthy habits, enough time, and smart financial guidance, you can become a millionaire.

In my counseling experience, too many people focus on looking wealthy and spend too little time building a life of wealth. You don't need a million dollars to have a rich life. Focus your investments in the areas where you'll receive the greatest return as you work toward your personal goals.

## Playing with Fire?

You may not want to wait many years for retirement and you may invest heavily or sacrifice your standard of living during your younger years. The Financial Independence, Retire Early (FIRE) movement is a program of extreme savings and investment that allows proponents to retire far earlier than traditional budgets and retirement savings would allow.

By dedicating up to 70% of income to savings and investments, followers of the FIRE movement may eventually quit their jobs and live solely off small withdrawals from their portfolios decades before the conventional retirement age of sixty-five.

Retiring early has its own challenges. It's possible to outlive your money. Financial risks aside, many retirees struggle to find meaningful activity, which can lead to anxiety or depression. The initial excitement may wear off after the first few months.

There is always the possibility of losing money when investing. With high-risk possibilities, we often blur the line between gambling and investing. When you play the Lottery or poker, it's very unlikely you'll win. While both can be exciting and entertaining, it's likely you'll lose money. I've heard gamblers justify their wagers as investing. There's a reason that programs like Gamblers Anonymous and Debtors Anonymous exist. I remember working with a client who literally lost his house at a casino. He had a gambling addiction and bet everything he owned. There is a thrill that comes with the possibility of huge financial gains.

*Day trading*, or buying and selling a security within the same day, isn't investing. Some people make money day trading. But let's consider the facts and the likelihood that any individual will make money. Multiple studies show very few day traders earn any amount of money after trading fees.[111]

When the market goes up, people are vocal about their success and make themselves sound like geniuses. Not as many share their failures, though losses occur frequently. Conversations on the site Reddit fueled trades of AMC and GameStop. A few traders on the social communication site encouraged buying shares of select stocks. Some traders made money, but others lost many millions of dollars in the frenzy. When you play with fire, there's a chance you'll get burned. Safety is all about managing the flame.

Many strategies exist with investing. Education and qualified professionals acting as fiduciaries can help guide you. This book does not provide specific investment strategies. The goal is to further your education and expose you to some different ways of thinking about your personal situation so that you can clarify your beliefs, financial personality, and goals.

## Is Investing in a Home Positive or Negative?

While some people have fallen victim to the buy-a-house-at-any-cost mentality, other people have amassed tremendous wealth through real estate. My neighbor John grew his small empire by starting as a self-employed rehabber and bought his first home as a fixer-upper. He then implemented the buy, repair, rent, refinance, and repeat (BRRRR) strategy.

John's goal was to generate positive cash flow so that he didn't have to rely on his physical labor as he aged. His properties were assets. The key was that he understood the math and had the tools to generate positive cash flow. In the meantime, his assets, the properties, also appreciated in value.

Stories of real estate moguls and epic failures are extremes. Most investors fall somewhere in the middle. If real estate is your thing, go after it. It can be a great way to build wealth, though it has its own risks.

One risk in real estate investing is that not all properties produce cash flow and not all homes appreciate in value. The latter is true when accounting for the cost of renovations. Maybe you've experienced the frustration of owning a home in need of endless repairs. It's an altogether different matter to understand the business of real estate.

You have likely heard that we calculate net worth by subtracting liabilities from assets. Now, there is some disagreement about the definitions of assets and liabilities. Take, for instance, a primary home. Some financial advisers will say that buying a home is the best investment you can make. Policymakers have a significant homeownership bias toward carrying a mortgage on a primary residence. We see this in plans like first-time homeownership programs with various incentives such as low down payments, no private mortgage insurance (PMI), down payment help, to name a few. There is also the ever-popular mortgage interest deduction in the US tax code.

Millions of people consider homeownership *the* path to wealth. It is part of the "American Dream." Many people believe that owning a house is an excellent investment, important for raising a family, and many save as much as possible to make it come true.

The data about the benefits of owning a home is mixed in reality. Often real estate agents and financial institutions cite community stability when advocating for government intervention in the housing market. A Johns Hopkins University study tested direct and indirect effects of homeownership on children's cognitive achievement, behavior problems, and health. The researchers concluded, "We find little evidence of beneficial homeownership effects and suggest that previous analyses may have mistaken selection differences for the effect of homeownership itself."[112]

Without proper understanding about the ins and outs of owning a home, many consumers have fallen victim to unscrupulous scammers. I remember years ago, while working with the FDIC in Boston, one aggressive community-based organization that had a homeownership-for-all focus. The program was essentially a pyramid scheme where prospective homeowners paid monthly into a pot and waited until it was their turn to buy a house.

A separate group in Worcester, Massachusetts, gained trust by speaking Spanish and targeting non-English speakers in their mortgage scheme. The unsuspecting victims relied on cultural affinity and believed the scammers had customers' best interests at heart. In reality, what they were selling was a high-cost predatory loan product. The customers were distressed homeowners in search of relief.

Unfortunately, some businesses break the law in search of profit. These are only two examples of many. It is against the law to make people pay up front for mortgage help. Federal law prohibits companies from collecting fees until a homeowner has actually received an offer of relief from the lender and accepted it. This is called the Mortgage Assistance Relief Services (MARS) rule.

Much like car dealers who offer loans that extend car payments and raise hidden costs, many unscrupulous lenders misrepresent mortgage products to unsuspecting clients. They offer negative amortizing loans where the balance increases every month even as payments are made on time. Some lenders increase the term to fifty years to get a buyer into a home that otherwise puts their budget into deficit. The lender isn't taking into consideration household family expenses or home maintenance.

A home is more than a house. People make memories, both good and bad, there. It can provide emotional security. For some, a home is a financial nightmare. For others, a house can be a fantastic investment, but it is a personal decision and not "right or wrong." There are many rich people who rent and many who struggle to make ends meet who have a mortgage.

If you're considering buying a home to live in, may I suggest using a calculator to determine if the numbers work to your advantage? Check out this Rent vs. Buy Calculator: https://www.schwabmoneywise.com/tools-resources/rent-vs-buy-calculator.

## The Other "Coin"

Social media and technology have brought tremendous fluctuations to the world of investing. A well-known influencer can affect billions of dollars with one tweet or TikTok video. Dogecoin is a cryptocurrency created by software engineers as a joke. Its market capitalization high was more than $12 billion in 2023. Tesla founder Elon Musk is one vocal supporter of the digital coin that has roots in a meme.

Market capitalization, or market cap, is a fancy way of saying the total value of all shares, or in this case coins. If there were 20 million shares selling at $50 per share, that stock or coin would have a market cap of $1 billion.

On the flip side of digital assets, hundreds of billions of dollars were wiped out of crypto markets in early 2021 when Elon Musk tweeted that Tesla would stop allowing the use of Bitcoin to buy its cars.

Investors who went all in on Squid Coin seeking speculative fast money lost everything. *Squid Game* is a Netflix show that took pop culture by storm in late 2021. While they did not affiliate the digital coin with the epic series, it took advantage of brand recognition. The popular brand helped to propel the crypto "asset" by over 2000% in twenty-four hours. It was all very exciting as they theoretically made millionaires overnight.

Investigators discovered that the project was a scam on November 1, 2021, and investors lost millions of dollars. The creators took all the invested money and ran.[113]

Using blockchain technology for digital currency isn't likely to go away. For an overview, read *The Basics of Bitcoins and Blockchains* by Antony Lewis[114] or *The Bitcoin Standard: The Decentralized Alternative to Central Banking* by Saifedean Ammous.[115]

Technology has also enabled nonfungible tokens (NFTs), which are unique digital assets built on blockchains. We use the blockchain tech to verify ownership of things like videos, pictures, music, event tickets—the list of possibilities is endless. My son and millions of other gamers are familiar with the concept as they play popular games on Roblox. Users create and sell digital items on the platform. Before you dismiss the idea as "child's play," consider that the Roblox Corporation made $2.5 billion in 2022.

To debunk the NFT craze, Geoffrey Huntley, a software engineer, created a website that at the end of 2021 was "The Heist of the Century." His website contained every NFT available through the Ethereum and Solana blockchains. It was a massive 20 TB (that's terabytes) torrent. For context, with 1 TB you can store 250,000 photos taken with a 12 MP camera; 250 movies or 500 hours of HD video; or 6.5 million document pages, commonly stored as Microsoft Office files, PDFs, and presentations.[116]

NFTs, however, are much more than digital pictures. The textbook publisher Pearson plans to turn its titles into non-fungible tokens. The Dallas Mavericks are currently using the technology to incentivize fans to attend more games. They reward Mavs fans with a digital collectible for each game they attend. A four-bedroom house in Gulfport, Florida, sold for 210 Ethereum, about $654,310 as a nonfungible token. Gary Vaynerchuk even created an NFT membership-based dining club called the Flyfish Club (FFC).

Why, you might ask, would they do that?

Vaynerchuk explained how the membership could become an asset to the token holder by utilizing NFTs and can later be sold, transferred, or leased to others on the secondary market. By utilizing NFTs, FFC (Flyfish Club) can create a loyal, member-community that we can provide special experiences for. NFTs create new modernistic financial models, which will allow FFC to deliver an exceptional and sustainable product for years to come."[117]

Fluctuations, market uncertainty, and new tech all provide investor opportunities. On the flip side, blindly following advice can bring disaster. During the latter half of 2022, the cryptocurrency market lost nearly $2 trillion, more than half of its entire capitalization.

Regulation will develop around cryptocurrencies and digital assets. Scams will continue, and we need change to protect investors.

In 2022, the Biden administration issued an executive order on "Ensuring Responsible Development of Digital Assets." Focused on creating financial stability, protection, and inclusion, the order cited the $3 trillion digital asset market cap and the fact that 16% of American adults have used cryptocurrencies.[118] It remains to be seen how well the inter-agency coordination will benefit consumers; however, it establishes a focused effort on changing technologies.

## Your Investing Action Plan

There are outstanding books and resources on investing. You can earn degrees and study for the rest of your life. As your personal education continues, don't succumb to analysis paralysis. Saving and investing require action. Learn the fundamentals, strategize, and be sure to put your learning into practice.

Begin with a budget to determine how much you can afford to invest. Some people are ready to aggressively invest like those in the FIRE movement, while other people may invest with spare change. Comparing ourselves to other investors in "better" situations will likely be discouraging. We can only control our personal finances. Once you have a handle on your income and expenses, including emergency savings, you're ready to move on to the next step.

Diving into investing without knowledge and understanding is like jumping into a swimming pool without checking to see if there's water; it's really risky. You can test yourself with this free investor quiz: https://tools.finra.org/knowledge_quiz/. You can take additional quizzes and learn about investment professionals and more here: https://www.investor.gov/.

Once you have a solid understanding, choose your investment strategy and start investing as soon as possible. You can begin investing with your company's retirement plan. Not everyone has a company-sponsored plan. That's okay; there are many other options. You can open a brokerage account in less time than it takes to read this book.

I'm a fan of investing in broad stock market index mutual funds or electronically traded funds (ETFs). Index-tracking funds try to match the returns and price movements of an index, such as the S&P 500. The managers passively manage the funds and keep costs low.

I also enjoy some real estate investing. I like the tangible aspect and can wrap my head around the basics after spending some time in real estate development years ago. We can choose from a plethora of assets to invest in, though none yields a better return than the investment in our own education and personal development.

You might be comfortable with risk and have an entrepreneurial disposition. Many people put everything they have into building businesses. Small businesses actually contribute almost 50% of the gross domestic product in the US. It's not for the faint of heart, but this is a significant area of wealth generation.

## Invest in Yourself and Glow Up

Be sure to invest with your head and not your emotions. Some smart people make awful investors because they're very emotional. Being mindful and in control will help you make rational investments as you build a wealthy life. How we invest our time has a tremendous impact on the quality of our lives and on our financial situations.

We could make an almost endless list of items with investing opportunities. Relationships, the environment, professional development, and personal health (physical, spiritual, and emotional) are just a few. Investing isn't random; it takes careful thought, research, planning, and perseverance to reap a reward.

Eating healthy foods and exercising is an investment in our physical well-being. There's a cost associated with an unhealthy lifestyle. Harvard research concluded that unhealthy eating habits cost the American health care system about $300 per person or $50 billion per year in medical costs just for heart-related diseases.[119]

The best investment strategy is always PERSONAL. It's custom tailored to our risk tolerance and goals. Don't be afraid to ask for help. Remember, it's dangerous to invest in assets and strategies we don't understand. Hire an adviser or coach. Network with people outside of your current circle. Read. And read some more. Plans with many advisers are more likely to succeed. Ask successful friends and family for advice. As you ask more questions, your knowledge will increase. With greater knowledge, you can ask better questions. Better questions lead to better answers.

Investing can be scary and overwhelming. Determine one thing you can do today to invest in your future. Just one thing, and do it. Successful people don't wait for more money, time, ambition, or anything else before we choose to build the life we want. Successful people invest always. Not just when it's convenient, or perfect, or after we break old habits, or for instant gratification, or when there is no fear. Courage is pressing toward our goals, despite the fear.

Dream big, persist, and you will shine brighter than you ever thought possible.

# MONEY TALK Q&A

## Q: Why is interest so important?

A: Consider the rule of 72 to help you consider how quickly interest affects money. The equation is this: 72 divided by the annual percentage rate (APR) of interest equals the number of years to double your money. Consider you have $5,000 earning 5% annually. In a little over fourteen years, you'd have $10,000.

Now consider having to pay interest using a credit card with a $5,000 balance and 30% APR. If you never used the account and made $150 monthly payments, it would take you over six years to pay the balance. You'd end up paying $10,884, which includes $5,884 in interest.

## Q: How much money should I save?

A: It depends. Many gurus will give a specific number. For example, you need to save at least 10% of your gross monthly income. I believe there is danger in overgeneralization. It's beneficial to create a budget and determine goals, which includes doing the math to determine what it'll take to reach the goals. The FIRE (Financial Independence, Retire Early) movement suggests saving between 25% and 50% of your after-tax income to allow you to retire in less than twenty years.

Either way, having savings to cover emergencies is crucial. If you've been getting deeper into debt, working toward savings while aggressively paying down debt could be a worthy goal.

For help with saving, check out:

- America Saves (https://americasaves.org/)
- Military Saves (https://militarysaves.org/)
- Consumer Financial Protection Bureau (https://www .consumerfinance.gov/start-small-save-up/)

## Q: Should I wait until all of my debt is paid off before I save or invest?

A: In most situations, no. The goal with credit card debt is to pay balances in full each month. If you have significant debt, it'll likely take years to pay the balances in full. The faster the debts are paid, the less interest you'll pay. It's quite possible that unexpected expenses will come up over the few years of paying what you owe. Emergency savings will help you avoid new debt.

## Q: When should I start investing?

A: As soon as possible. Consider this example from three different investors, Dawn, Lonnie, and Sara. All three earn the same 7% annual rate of return on their investment funds. The only difference is when and how often they save.

Dawn invests $5,000 per year, beginning at age eighteen. At age twenty-eight, she stops. She has invested for ten years and has contributed $50,000 total.

Lonnie invests the same $5,000 but begins where Dawn left off. He begins investing at age twenty-eight and continues the annual $5,000 investment until he retires at age fifty-eight. Lonnie has invested for thirty years and has put in $150,000 total.

Sara invests $5,000 per year beginning at age eighteen and continues investing until retirement at age fifty-eight. She has invested for forty years and has set aside $200,000.

At the retirement age of fifty-eight, Dawn has accumulated $602,070; Lonnie has $540,741; and Sara has a whopping $1,142,811.

Lonnie has invested three times as much money as Dawn, yet Dawn's account has a higher value. She saved for only ten years, while Lonnie saved for thirty years. This example illustrates the power of compound interest; the investment return that Dawn earned in her ten early years of saving is snowballing. The effect is so drastic that Lonnie can't catch up, even if he saves for an additional twenty years.

## Q: How do I invest if I'm under eighteen?

A: In order for a minor to invest (or if you're opening an account for a minor), it's necessary to have a custodial account. Research your options to determine what's best for you. Here are a couple of places to get started:

- Fidelity (www.fidelity.com/go/youth-account/overview)
- Acorns (https://www.acorns.com/)

## Q: How much money do I need to invest?

A: Less than you might think. It's possible to invest with spare change on a platform with low-cost options like:

- Acorns (https://www.acorns.com/)
- Fidelity (www.fidelity.com)
- Schwab (www.schwab.com)

## Q: How much can I withdraw from my portfolio without depleting my savings over a long retirement?

A: The general rule has been about 4% of retirement savings annually. Many advisers use this number because it assumes that their clients will withdraw the same amount every year and will continue earning over 4% on their stocks and bonds. While the rule may be an okay place to start, it's helpful to personalize your spending rate. Here are a few questions to get you thinking:

What other assets or income do you have? If you have a pension, defined benefit plan, other savings, inheritance, annuities, or other sources of retirement income, you may not need to touch your portfolio beyond taking the minimum distribution.

How long are you planning for? I know, trying to determine life expectancy is morbid. There's a big difference between retiring when you're thirty versus seventy.

What will your asset allocation be? If all of your retirement funds are in savings or certificate of deposit accounts, the yield will probably be far less than 4%. Consider your risk tolerance so you don't lose sleep.

Will you have large expenses? Preexisting health conditions can affect retirement. Do you have property to maintain? Will family members rely on your generosity?

How can you ensure flexibility in your financial plans? (Change is inevitable.)

### Q: How do I learn my risk tolerance for investing?

A: Check out the free risk tolerance assessment from the University of Missouri (https://pfp.missouri.edu/research/investment -risk-tolerance-assessment/).

### Q: Where can I find helpful investing resources?

A: Investor.gov (https://www.investor.gov/) has investing quizzes, tools, and plenty of resources.

## Q: I have a basic understanding about investing. How can I learn even more?

A: Consider college-level finance courses. You can take free high-quality courses through Coursera (https://www.coursera .org/courses?query=investment) or edX (https://www.edx.org /learn/investing).

## Q: Where should I invest my money?

A: It would be irresponsible for me to give an answer in a few sentences. If you consider hiring an adviser, ask if they're a fiduciary to ensure they have your best interests in mind (as opposed to being a salesperson). BrokerCheck (https://brokercheck.finra .org/) is a free tool to research the background and experience of brokers, advisers, and firms. FINRA also has educational publications such as "How to Find and Work with an Investment Professional" and more.

There are many paths to financial freedom, though many famous personalities may tell you that their way is the only way. Educate yourself. Create a plan. Keep it simple. Stick to it. Adjust the course as necessary. Peter Lynch, a famous investor, mutual fund manager, and philanthropist, said, "Never invest in any idea you can't illustrate with a crayon."[120]

For more on investing, instant access to an Identify Your Money Type tool, an Investment Risk Tolerance Quiz, and courses on cryptocurrencies, visit www.MattParadise.com/capablebonus.

# 14

## TO YOUR CREDIT

### More Than Just a Score

A few years ago, a young single father in a dire situation sought my help. Kevin worked long hours driving for Uber, but because of past mistakes and misfortunes, he was suffering extreme consequences. Out of necessity, he leased a basic Camry from Uber for more than $1,200 per month. To put that in perspective, with a perfect credit record, you can finance a new sedan for less than $400.

Kevin had fallen behind on a few bills when he was nineteen years old. The delinquencies caused a chain reaction that, a few years later, led to couch-surfing and struggling to feed his daughter, Noelle. His credit history prevented him from obtaining a reasonable car loan and even an apartment.

A young woman I counseled insisted on impressing the world with her outfits. Sarah had boxes of shoes stacked from floor to ceiling in her small apartment. She had tremendous fashion sense, but her shopping compulsion led her to accumulate tens of thousands of dollars in credit card debt.

There's a decent chance you've heard a horror story about debt. Maybe you've had your own personal struggles. You might have used credit cards for the perks and rewards or relied on credit to improve your comfort or supplement your lifestyle.

Borrowing can feel like the simple solution to being stuck in that place between saving money and living life with unrestrained enthusiasm and zeal. However, credit cards can be debt traps for many, many people.

If you find navigating credit confusing, you're not alone. Yes, even many so-called professionals don't agree on the fundamentals.

I remember sitting in on a lecture in Boston conducted by a large, reputable financial services company headquartered in the area. The talk wasn't particularly exciting until the presenter mentioned incorrect details about credit reporting. The blatant untruth made my skin crawl, and though it was uncomfortable for both me and the presenter, I stood and kindly corrected him in front of a packed auditorium. Accurate information was necessary for the seminar participants, who were service providers receiving training, to assist their clients with personal finance.

Just because someone has recognized credentials, licenses, or experience doesn't mean that their teaching is accurate. I truly believe that the presenter meant no harm, but the mistake would have carried immeasurable consequences. If you're wondering if this statement is overly dramatic, it's not.

Credit affects your ability to get and keep a job. Credit affects your ability to get housing and affordable insurance rates, and more! Yes, credit is as important as it is controversial and misunderstood.

People make mistakes. I've made plenty in my personal and professional life and have learned from them. For this reason, a useful saying is, "Trust, but verify."

## The Good, the Bad, and the Ugly

When most people refer to "good" or "bad" credit, they're referring to a three-digit score designed to assess an individual's ability to repay debt. Credit is much broader than that. Let's start with a basic understanding of credit by first defining different types.

First, but in no particular order, is *revolving credit*. If you've ever used a credit card, then you're familiar with the concept. It's a type of credit in which the consumer's balance and minimum monthly payment can fluctuate, and where the cardholder can avoid finance charges by paying the statement balance within the grace period.

Examples include Home Equity Lines of Credit (HELOCs) and retail credit cards from business such as department stores or gas stations. Revolving accounts don't automatically close when the account reaches a zero balance; they remain open for use until the lender or the consumer closes the accounts. Yes, the lender can close an account for any reason. Account inactivity and going over the account's borrowing limit are the primary reasons an account might be closed.

Unlike a revolving credit card, a charge card is a *non-installment credit*. Consumers repay the amount borrowed in a short amount of time, often within thirty days. If a person fails to pay the charge card balance in full by the due date, the interest rate will default to a high rate like 30% APR. One example of this type of account is American Express.

Another common type of credit is *installment credit*. Using installment credit (or an installment account/installment loan), the consumer borrows a certain amount of money and agrees to pay it back over a fixed period. A car loan is a prime example of installment credit. If John borrows $30,000 to buy a new car, the lender might set his payments at $665 per month for forty-eight months. That means that over the next forty-eight months, John's payments will equal $31,920. The $30,000 is the principal and the extra $1,920 is the interest.

Popular types of installment loans include auto loans, home mortgages, student loans, and personal loans, which people use for debt consolidation, large purchases, or even emergencies.

Many people lack the savings to buy new living room, dining room, or bedroom furniture. While a $5,000 price tag is prohibitive, a smaller number, say $150 per month, is likely more approachable. Most auto dealerships advertise their vehicles by the monthly payment, since few households can afford $40,000. I have friends with six-figure incomes who consider a monthly car payment a foregone conclusion, making it much easier for the auto dealers to keep upgrading their clients to a new vehicle every few years. This mentality helps account for the nearly 17 million new vehicles sold in the US every year.

Car dealers are notorious for upselling and for manipulating numbers by varying the loan interest rates and increasing the number of years/payments on the loans. Salespeople use these variables to close deals and increase profits. If you're going to finance a vehicle, plan for that separately from the price negotiation.

You can search for loan terms to find the best interest rate and then negotiate the price of the vehicle. Search online at sites such as www.Edmunds.com and www.kelleybluebook.com to find information such as the dealer cost, the sticker price, and the average price paid for a vehicle.

With installment loans, it's crucial to understand the term length of the loan and the fees, including interest. Read the fine print. With mortgages, there may be additional stipulations, such as prepayment penalties. As I mentioned earlier in this book, mortgages can even be negatively amortizing, so your monthly payment doesn't even cover the interest, and the balance actually increases each month. While the Dodd-Frank legislation limited some predatory lending practices in 2008, they still exist.

A fourth type of credit is *service credit*. Examples include phone bills, utility bills, and cable bills. Many service providers do not charge interest and most do not report on-time payments to credit bureaus. This reporting is neutral-negative, which addresses the common question, "I pay all my bills on time; why isn't my credit score higher?" However, they report missed payments, which are harmful to your credit.

The last type of credit falls under the umbrella of *high-risk credit*. Examples of high-risk lenders include payday lenders, pawn shops, and refund-anticipation loans. Maybe you've heard a slogan like "buy here, pay here" or "no credit, no problem." Some borrowers turn to these companies for emergency short-term relief. With a payday loan, for example, a customer can write a post-dated check to the lender for the amount of their salary and immediately receive cash. While the loans are convenient, they're very expensive and difficult to repay.

Several years ago, a few friends and I collaborated with the FDIC in Massachusetts and Texas to develop a quick reference guide to understanding high-cost financial services, products, and mainstream banking alternatives. We aimed the guide toward community organizations and practitioners, though it's relevant for consumers.

You can download the entire publication by visiting www.MattParadise.com/capablebonus.

Use caution if a loan product or transaction service features one or more of these elements. Avoid any lender who:

- Bases loan approval on the debtor's assets, rather than on their ability to repay,

- Encourages the borrower to refinance rather than pay off a loan so that the lender can charge additional fees,

- Tries to conceal the true cost of the loan product from an unsuspecting or unsophisticated borrower (hiding information may indicate fraudulent or deceptive practices),

- Charges excessive fees and/or interest rates beyond those that would cover a lender's risk and profitable return,

- Undertakes fraudulent, high-pressure, or misleading marketing and sales efforts,

- Shows evidence of abusive collection practices, or

- Aggressively solicits residents of low-income or minority neighborhoods or other vulnerable populations.

Two significant defenses against shady business practices are education and consumer protection laws. One of my past roles was to lobby and advocate for consumer protections. Connecticut, Georgia, Maine, Maryland, Massachusetts, New Jersey, New York, North Carolina, Pennsylvania, Vermont, and West Virginia are among the few exemplary states that continue to maintain strong usury laws and to enforce those laws, limiting the impact of predatory lending on their citizens.

The state governments have curbed the predatory activity in these states with powerful protections. To be clear, *curbed* is different from prevented. Georgia enacted a tough anti-payday loan law to close loopholes and strengthen penalties against lenders that exceed the state's 60% usury cap. You read that correctly, 60% interest.

The other thirty-nine states have legalized payday lending using provisions, such as mandatory databases, cooling-off periods, attempts to stop rollovers and back-to-back transactions, and attempts to stop people from borrowing from multiple lenders. However, even with the addition of all these measures to slow consumers from over-borrowing, these laws do not stop the debt trap.

On a recent business trip to Arizona, I took mental note of the number of financial institutions between the airport and my short ride to the hotel. The predatory lenders and service providers vastly outnumbered the mainstream businesses. Payday lenders, pawnbrokers, and other predatory lenders were everywhere. If you think a 60% annual percentage rate is high, consider that some predatory loans have rates that often exceed 400%.

## Like a Diamond, Credit Has Cs

With a quick Google search, you'll find a range of three to twelve Cs regarding getting credit. A couple of reasons for the variance are the overlapping use of terms and international considerations. I've always used five Cs to help understand creditworthiness, and I'll outline them here.

### Capacity or Cash Flow

The first element of creditworthiness is capacity, or cash flow, which represents sufficient income each month to meet obligations.

Fun fact: Your credit score doesn't consider your income, so the amount of money you make doesn't show up on your traditional credit report.

However, lenders will consider your ability to repay a loan by calculating your debt-to-income (DTI) ratio. They calculate the ratio by dividing total ongoing monthly debt payments by monthly gross income.

Remember, just because a lender says you can afford a loan doesn't mean the math of your actual budget in line with their decision. DTI doesn't account for living expenses such as groceries and clothing for your family. There's only way to truly know your cash flow and whether you can afford additional debt. Yup, that dirty B word.

### Capital

For personal loans, a lender may want to see a certain amount of money in your accounts. The balance in your savings, investment, or other accessible accounts is capital. A lender can consider the capital as a backup to pay a debt if you have cash flow issues. The capital also lowers the lender's risk because when a borrower's own money is on the line, it provides a sense of ownership and an incentive to repay the loan.

Money in the bank also shows how well someone is managing their finances. When we have money in the bank, it shows our ability to budget and manage cash flow beyond living paycheck-to-paycheck.

If we're barely making ends meet from month to month, a minor setback could derail our entire life. To a lender or even a landlord, this could signal the possibility of not getting paid.

Landlords manage risk by asking for a security deposit. If you've never had credit before, you may be required to give them a cash deposit to be held as collateral.

A mortgage lender may require you to put a certain percentage down and cover closing costs from your personal savings.

They may even ask for several months of bank statements to ensure that you've been consistently putting money away. The down payment is your vested interest, your equity in the property, and your collateral for the loan.

## Collateral

Collateral is an asset accepted as security in order to lower risk. If car loan payments are missed, the lender can repossess the vehicle. A pawn shop will hold your valuables for a period in exchange for a loan. If you have a mortgage, the collateral is the home. Lenders don't want your home; they want your money so they can lend it and earn more money. To a borrower, a mortgage represents more than a loan. It represents the home where memories are made. It could be a cash-flowing asset at the center of financial independence.

Someone with a poor credit history may resort to a high-risk loan, such as a title loan, which comes with a high interest rate and your vehicle on the line. If you miss payments, then the vehicle belongs to the lender, even if the value is greater than the amount you owe. When lenders use a person's house or car as collateral, they have a greater assurance that the loan will be repaid.

Collateral creates the difference between two types of debt: secured and unsecured. The debt becomes secured when collateral is required.

## Conditions

This C of credit encompasses both the loan specifics and broader economic conditions. Loan terms include the purpose of a loan, the amount, and the interest rate. The state of the economy,

Financially Capable

overall industry trends, or changes to legislation can all affect
your ability to get a loan.

Landlords may adjust rent based on supply and demand,
interest rates, inflation, tax, and other factors. During a recession,
credit card issuers may reduce available credit by closing accounts
or lowering individual credit limits. For more on credit conditions,
check out https://www.newyorkfed.org/outreach-and-education
/community-development/credit-conditions.

An individual's creditworthiness isn't considered in isolation.
It really is a relative assessment.

### Character

The last, but certainly not least C of credit, is character. What
comes to mind when you think about character? I've received
answers that range from traits such as honesty, trustworthiness,
and patience to the other end of the thought process where
superheroes and comic book characters land. When I follow up
and ask how all of that relates to credit, my audience members
often wear expressions similar to the one you might have while
reading this—a blank stare.

When we assess someone's character, we determine how
trustworthy and reliable we think they are.

Consider this example: A random stranger walks up to you
on the street and says, "You don't know me, but I really need to
borrow your car. It's an emergency. I'm reliable and trustworthy.
I'll fill up the tank before returning your vehicle. There won't be
a scratch on it, and I'll return it right on time. So, can I grab
your keys? You trust me, right?"

While I like to believe in the virtues of my fellow humans,
I subscribe to the saying "trust, but verify."

When we judge somebody's character, do we just listen to what they say? No. Talk is cheap. We want to see actions. Lenders consider many of the same traits. The various ways we've handled financial obligations show up on our credit reports, both the negative and the positive.

Character is arguably the most important C. Lenders are interested in an applicant's history and how we paid loans in the past. On a deeper level, character is about trust. If a family is renting one side of their two-unit home, they need to feel safe. They want to make sure their home is cared for and that the relationship with their neighbors is good.

An employer needs a productive and trustworthy employee. One hiring manager told me, "I evaluate credit reports when I consider hiring an employee. The report provides insight into how someone manages their finances, but it also gives me insight into their character."

As mentioned earlier, credit doesn't equal debt. There are many credit reporting agencies and many scores. They all vary in how they weigh the Cs, but all will consider these five: capacity, capital, collateral, conditions, and character.

## The Safety and Benefits of Credit Cards

Often, installment and revolving debts keep families living beyond their means. This can't go on indefinitely. I've counseled many households who didn't realize that high-interest credit cards subsidized their lifestyle. The adults called for help once they reached their credit limits, at which point they had to make tough decisions to work toward a positive monthly cash flow.

Sometimes the debt financed a business; other times unexpected medical expenses delivered a significant shock. Too often, debt financed a lavish lifestyle, possibly including coffee with friends, an outing to a movie theater, a nicer car, or dining out to enjoy favorite foods. For some parents, the necessity of buying clothes for kids became, "That is too cute! I need that outfit for my child."

Some well-known personalities recommend avoiding debt and credit altogether. Their stance is that everyone should buy everything with cash and, when that's not possible, use debit cards. That advice is foolish and even reckless.

We live in a credit-based society. Building credit can help with building a career; many employers check credit in the employment screening process. We can leverage credit to build wealth, such as an investment in real estate. It plays a critical role when renting an apartment. We use credit for renting cars and for traveling. Yes, you can rent a hotel room without a credit card, but make sure you have enough money to cover your hotel stay, all the required deposits, and your general living expenses for a week or more after you leave the hotel. The "hold" on debit cards may be higher than if you were to use a revolving card.

Credit is an area where I believe "personal" should remain prominent. I've worked with some individuals who have never once used credit cards or loans. I have friends who choose to live off the grid and produce everything they consume. On the flip side, many financial empires have been built using credit. I'm not judging one way or the other, though I have my preference.

If your ideal life is one where you don't need financial products, services, or modern amenities, go for it. In fact, many people do. It's quite possible to live a happy, healthy life doing so. Personally, that's not the life my family chooses. If it's not the life you choose, I'd suggest that you keep an open mind and educate yourself about living in a credit-based economy.

I recommend using a credit card over a debit card. (*That does not mean carrying a balance. The goal with credit cards is to pay the balance in full every month.*) One reason is for superior fraud protection. The Electronic Fund Transfer Act (EFTA) protects consumers when they transfer funds. This includes the use of debit cards, automated teller machines (ATMs), and automatic withdrawals from a bank account. It's important to recognize that you may still be responsible for fraud or theft from your account.

If there are unauthorized withdrawals from a card that is lost or stolen, consider:

- They limit total loss to $500 if you notify the financial institution within two business days.

- Your loss could be up to $5,000 if you notify the institution between three and fifty-nine days.

- If you do not report the loss within sixty business days, you risk an unlimited loss on transfers made after the sixty-day period—you could lose all the money in the account plus maximum overdraft fees, if any.

Most credit cards offer zero liability and the companies monitor accounts for fraudulent activity. When there is unauthorized use, someone is stealing from the financial institution, and the company uses their resources to resolve the issue. When there's fraudulent activity on a debit account, it's your money. In my experience, the institution is far less motivated to replace the money in your account.

At the very least, if you choose to use debit cards for purchases, monitor your account frequently.

Besides safety, credit cards often provide additional benefits. Account rewards can be significant. I have a friend who charged almost everything, including his mortgage, every month. He needed to make the house payment, and he planned for it in his budget. Charging his mortgage payment on his credit card allowed him to reap massive airline miles.

Personally, in our household, we use a few cards within a month. We have one that we use only for gas and we receive a 5% rebate at gas stations in addition to any other incentives. We use another card that gives us 5% back on groceries. Our card literally pays us when we use it to buy the food we budgeted for. Though it's easier said than done, the goal is to **pay credit card balances in full every single month** within the billing cycle. When you pay the entire balance before the due date, you avoid interest charges.

If you can only afford the minimum payment, then the card is subsidizing your lifestyle. I understand that sometimes we use cards for emergencies, such as auto repairs or medical expenses. Credit card interest is brutal long-term.

CareCredit is a popular medical credit card offered by many medical offices during the visit. Dentists, chiropractors, and veterinarians are examples of where you might find the card accepted. If a dentist tells you that you need a procedure to avoid life-threatening consequences, you'll try to make it happen. If you don't have the cash or credit available on another card, the healthcare provider may offer you the convenience of a CareCredit card on the spot. While convenient, the cards usually come with a 26.99% annual percentage rate.

Let's do some quick math. If you have a $5,000 dental bill and make a monthly payment that includes interest plus 1% every month with a 27% APR, it'll take about 290 months to pay the balance in full. If you thought the bill was high, the total you'll end up paying is more than $10,500. While compounding is great for saving and investing, it's terrible when you have to pay interest.

If you're not convinced by these benefits alone, there are more benefits to using credit cards over debit cards for purchases. Let's not underestimate convenience. If you ever rent a hotel room, a credit card is the way to go. Using a debit card for a hotel room isn't wise for several reasons. The biggest one is that many of us don't have enough money in our accounts to cover room rates, taxes, and the temporary deposit for incidentals. With a credit card, the incidentals deposit is a hold on your credit card. But with a debit card, the money in your bank account is reduced, and it could take up to a week for the hotel to give it back.

Most gas stations also place a hold on your account when you pay with a debit card, and the amount of the hold often exceeds the amount of gas you purchase. If you're not careful, this hold can lead to account overdraw and costly fees.

Renting a car with a debit card can present challenges too. Rental companies place a hold for the estimated charges of the rental and, in addition, can request an extra hold based on certain factors they deem appropriate. They may get additional authorizations from your account to cover the rental. These charges may include (but are not limited to) a cleaning fee and an extra fee for extending the rental period.

Here's the last, but not least, reason I prefer to use credit cards. Often, the rental agency will run a credit inquiry when you pay by debit card. This can cause a "hard" inquiry on your credit report. Hard inquiries lower credit scores. There are other pros and cons to credit versus debit, but I think I've made a pretty good case.

An important note: Just because your debit card has a Mastercard or Visa logo and you choose "credit" at the point of sale or transaction doesn't mean you're paying with credit. It refers to the payment process method, and your bank or credit union may charge you additional fees.

The convenience, safety, and benefits of credit cards aren't the only reason I disagree with an anti-credit stance. Credit does not equal debt. Credit is much broader and more significant in our largely credit-based economy than credit cards or credit scores.

## The Downside of Using Credit Cards

So, is credit important and if so, why?

I'll say, first, an emphatic yes. Credit enables our economy to function. Many businesses rely on credit to operate. As we've established, you've likely used or are using some type of credit even if you don't use revolving accounts. If you have a cell phone, internet, electricity, or indoor plumbing, you're using forms of service credit.

You're probably familiar with some negative aspects of borrowing. As a credit counselor, I spoke with people daily who were drowning in debt. It was common for people to call the office with six figures in credit card debt. Few called for education or strategies to avoid financial difficulties, even though the counseling was free.

The most revolving debt I remember one person having was just over $500,000, all on credit cards charging more than a 25% APR. It's too easy to accumulate debt. Consider findings from a February 2021 MIT report that examined the neuroscience of buying things:

- Using credit cards stimulates the brain's reward system and an urge for further spending.

- People were more willing to buy more expensive items with credit than cash and spent more overall when using a credit card.

- When people bought things with a credit card, brain scans using an MRI revealed that the striatum, a region of the brain's reward system, was activated. The striatum releases dopamine, a hormone involved in reward, reinforcement, pleasure, and even addiction.[121]

## Important for Jobs

With a warning about the debt trap, let's consider ways we use credit beyond the possibility of debt. First, many employers consider an applicant's credit when they hire. According to the Professional Background Screening Association (PBSA), 95% of companies conduct some type of background check on potential employees—the majority, 51% pull credit or financial checks on all job candidates.[122]

The largest employer in the United States, the military, considers the credit of their employees, not only during the hiring process, but also throughout their career. A service member can lose their security clearance and their job, based on what appears on their credit report.

In introducing this book, I told you about "Stephen," a high-ranking member of the military. He was very clear that our conversation needed to be confidential because the mere act of speaking with a credit counselor about unmanageable debt was a security threat. He had the genuine concern of losing his job over the accumulated debt. Fortunately, we created a workable plan to manage cash flow, pay down debt, reduce interest rates, and save his career.

You might be one of millions of people who consider such practices invasive. Layering on top of concerns of "none of your business" is the fact that many credit reports have errors. Consumer Reports found that more than one-third of consumers have errors on their reports.[123]

Politicians have proposed to overhaul the system of credit reporting. While it's unlikely that a new public credit reporting agency will eliminate the existing companies anytime soon, it puts the need for reform in the spotlight. If you think a credit report is out of bounds for a potential employer to see, it's just the beginning.

Consider the awe and disbelief of one of my high school classes. I had the privilege of working with them while serving on the board of a nonprofit that taught career pathways and provided education, academic support, and internships to inner-city youth.

One group of students in East Boston was interested in criminal justice. I brought on a friend who trained recruits at the Boston Police Department for twenty-plus years. He explained to the students that, when applying to the academy, the BPD considers many factors. He highlighted the importance of being "one person"—the same person at home, at school, and out in public. Even when accepted into the police training academy, they can kick the recruit out if there is questionable content on their social media.

This idea sparked some spirited debate, since it appalled many students that their actions in their personal lives could affect their careers.

You might ask why an employer cares about your credit report or social media. While training a group of hiring managers, I asked for their personal opinions for additional insight. One participant said that, for her company, the credit report showed the character of an individual: "The report shows if they were responsible with their money and if they paid bills on time or not. If the employee is having trouble with their finances, then they may have problems on the job. They could have trouble focusing, and the stress of debt could reduce productivity."

If you don't want to lose the opportunity for your dream job, you would be wise to ensure that your credit report is the best it can be. While careers are one significant reason credit is important, they're not the only reason.

## Important for Shelter

Another significant reason to maintain a strong credit rating is for housing. For sure, credit matters when getting a loan of any type, including a mortgage. But even if you're not interested in buying a home, landlords in search of the perfect tenant use credit reports to weed out potential renters. Landlords want to understand the character of their tenants because they want to gauge trustworthiness.

In providing education and counseling to individuals and families in homeless shelters, I also provided training for employees of social service agencies. The train-the-trainer model was critical because in prior years, the rehousing agents would work tirelessly, sometimes for years with a client, only to find out that a landlord wouldn't rent to an individual. Sometimes the landlord was willing, but a past due utility bill showed up on a credit report and impeded a lease.

## Important for Safety

Another reason for understanding credit and reporting is personal safety. Domestic violence shelters are an unfortunate necessity. It breaks my heart that domestic violence exists in the first place, and the violence has increased during the COVID-19 pandemic.[124]

It's possible for abusers to find personal information on credit reports. Creditors, utility companies, and other entities who run the reports update current addresses. Economic entanglement, or a compromising relationship, makes it difficult for survivors to leave an abuser and be self-sufficient. It forces some to return to unsafe situations for economic reasons.

The following resources provide information on credit and credit scoring and provide survivors with tools to obtain economic self-sufficiency.

Center for Survivor Agency & Justice (www.csaj.org) is a national organization dedicated to enhancing advocacy for survivors of intimate partner violence. The organization has made available recordings and presentations with topics such as credit reporting and repair for survivors, credit checks (as a barrier to employment), and the use of identity theft by domestic violence perpetrators.

National Resource Center on Domestic Violence (https://vawnet.org/sc/credit) offers a free resource library on gender-based violence.

If you or someone you know is at risk for domestic violence, here are additional resources:

- Domestic Shelters (www.domesticshelters.org/)
- Women's Law (www.womenslaw.org/find-help /advocates-and-shelters)
- National Domestic Violence Hotline (www.thehotline.org/), 1-800-799-SAFE (7233), or TTY 1-800-787-3224
- National Sexual Assault Hotline, 1-800-656-HOPE

An abuser can monitor internet usage and it's impossible to clear your browser's history completely. If you're concerned that someone might check your web access, call a toll-free hotline for help.

## Important for Protection

The last reason I'll list to illustrate the importance of credit is for insurance. In all but a few states, a low credit score will probably increase your insurance premiums. You could have a perfect driving record and still have an increased car insurance premium because of your credit. The Federal Trade Commission found in an independent study that credit-based insurance scores are effective predictors of risk.

Credit can also affect other insurance costs, such as home, renters, and even life insurance. Notice how I said "credit" and not credit score? I mentioned that credit is much larger than just one three-digit number. So many terms: credit, credit bureaus/ credit reporting agencies, credit reports, and credit scores. No wonder there's so much confusion.

# MONEY TALK Q&A

## Q: How can I build/establish credit?

A: Building credit can feel like a catch-22. To get it, you need to first have it. Don't despair—the following are a couple of tried-and-true ways to build credit:

1.  You can get a secured credit card or loan. This type of account usually costs more than an unsecured account, so be careful to read the fine print and consider if the expense is worthwhile. As an example, the vehicle secures a car loan. Using the loan to build credit will be expensive, particularly with the interest you'll pay. If you have a deposit account, your bank or credit union may have a credit-building product for you.

2.  Another way to build credit is to ask a family member or friend to put you on one or multiple accounts that they actively use. As long as they report the accounts to the three main credit bureaus, this will build your credit at no additional cost.

## Q: How do I fix credit report errors?

A: The process to fix errors often takes time. There are companies that will take your money for credit repair; be aware of the details. The company can't promise results and can be expensive. Consider the following resources to help correct errors:

*   Consumer Financial Protection Bureau
    (www.consumerfinance.gov/about-us/blog/common
    -errors-credit-report-and-how-get-them-fixed/)

- Federal Trade Commission (FTC)
  ( www.consumer.ftc.gov/articles/disputing-errors-your
  -credit-reports and www.consumer.ftc.gov/sites/default
  /files/articles/pdf/pdf-0034-credit-repair.pdf)

## Q: How do I fix bad credit?

A: There's not a quick fix or magic formula that will erase debt or negative information from your credit report. If you have debt, it's helpful to have a holistic view of the situation. Consider all debts, not just the one causing the most trouble. Consider assets and the household budget.

If you're considering the services of a credit counselor, this resource from the FTC is a good place to start: www.consumer .ftc.gov/articles/0153-choosing-credit-counselor.

You can find local credit counselors through the National Foundation for Credit Counseling (www.nfcc.org/).

## Q: What's the best way to pay off debt?

A: Start with a comprehensive plan that includes a budget. Account for every dollar of income, expenses, assets, and liabilities. The details matter. Experian (https://www.experian.com/blogs/ask-experian/credit-card-payoff-calculator/) has a credit card payoff calculator. For additional strategies, check out the FTC (www .consumer.ftc.gov/articles/getting-out-debt).

To receive free credit-related resources such as information on the use of credit in employment, visit www.MattParadise.com/capablebonus.

# 15

## DON'T JUDGE ME;
## IT'S ONLY THREE DIGITS

One of the most expensive aspects of debt is the shame, guilt, and anxiety that often accompany the money owed. In her novel *Evermore*, Alyson Noël wrote, "Forgiveness is healing . . . especially forgiving yourself."[125] Some of you need empathy and healing. If debt is your reality, embrace the opportunity to build discipline. Allow yourself grace. Seek help as needed.

I met Kim while volunteering at a local anti-poverty agency. She was a young woman who aged out of foster care, which happens when someone graduates from high school or turns eighteen. She became homeless immediately.

Kim had less-than-perfect credit. Even though she never used credit cards, she had delinquent student loans. While striving to become self-sufficient, she pursued her education. Unfortunately, the for-profit school where she enrolled was one of many online programs that defrauded students. Despite the fraud, a collection agency persistently attempted to collect the tens of thousands of dollars in student loan debt. Even worse than her owing money was the fact that her school certificate was worthless.

Kim was overwhelmed with emotions due to the stress. When she tried to get a job or an apartment, she was told that her poor credit was the reason they denied her. The lack of academic credentials made it nearly impossible for her to earn a living wage.

During our first meeting, we reviewed her credit report and developed a strategy to deal with the student loans. It took about eight months, but we had the debt forgiven and removed from her report. Kim was excited beyond words the day a landlord accepted her rental application. That day, Kim took one huge, hopeful step toward stability and self-sufficiency.

Unfortunately, Kim's story of struggle is not unique. Teenagers who age out of foster care are at high risk for becoming homeless during the transition to self-sufficiency. A national study found about 38% of "aged-out" young adults had been homeless at least once by age twenty-six.[126]

## Who's Reporting What?

Now that we have a solid basic understanding about credit and its importance, let's dive deeper to learn about reporting and scoring.

A credit reporting agency (CRA), or credit bureau, is a business that maintains historical and personal finance-related information about individuals and businesses. Compiling information from all different sources such as lenders, employers, landlords, and utility companies, the agencies produce a report. The three most well-known credit bureaus are Equifax, Experian, and TransUnion.

Getting a credit report is critical for everyone, even if you're not applying for a loan. One reason to review your report is for early fraud detection. Here's why. A few years ago, Melissa came to me for help. She was paying her bills, but her loan applications were getting denied and she was receiving odd notices from the IRS. We pulled her credit report and found multiple jobs reported in states where she had never lived. We followed the information and found that another woman was using Melissa's social security number.

If you've never seen your report, or it's been a while, go do it. It's free by law.

To order your credit report, visit www.AnnualCreditReport .com, or call (877) 322-8228. You may order your reports from each of the three nationwide credit reporting companies at once, or you can order your report from each of the companies one at a time.

UPDATE: Because of the COVID-19 pandemic, everyone in the US can get six free credit reports per year through 2026 by visiting the Equifax website, www.equifax.com, or by calling (866) 349-5191. That's in addition to the one free Equifax report (plus your Experian and TransUnion reports) you can get at www.AnnualCreditReport.com.

## Beyond the Big Three

While the three listed agencies are the primary national CRAs, there are many more. For instance, ChexSystems is a large agency that provides account verification services. They collect and report data on checking account applications, openings, and closures, including reasons for account closure. I've had clients who had challenges opening a deposit account and the first step we took was to run the ChexSystems (www.chexsystems .com) report. You can get your report for free.

Other agencies have specific areas of attention. For instance, MIB, Inc., collects information about medical conditions and reports this information to life and health insurance companies to assess your risk and eligibility during the underwriting of individual life, health, disability, illness, and long-term care insurance policies. Milliman IntelliScript (www.rxhistories.com/) collects prescription drug purchase history to quantify the relative mortality risk of life insurance applicants.

Several other agencies specifically track low-income and subprime borrowers. Subprime just means an individual has less-than-perfect credit. The agencies collect consumer information for, and provide data to, payday lenders, rent-to-own businesses, furniture stores that offer financing, auto finance and leasing companies, high-risk consumer finance businesses, subprime home lending businesses, subprime card issuers, banks, credit unions, cable/telecom companies, and debt buyers/collectors.

Did you know that there are companies that monitor and report about retail product return and exchange fraud and abuse (www.signifyd.com/)? A retail company can decide that you've returned or exchanged too many items and stop you from doing so in the future.

## Not All History Is Nostalgic

There are pros and cons to our current system of credit. I had an employee who enjoyed regaling anyone who would listen about banking stories from the 1960s. "Back in the day" meant significant prejudice. Redlining, as I discussed earlier in this book, was common practice. Gender disparities were also rampant. Getting a loan as a single woman was all but impossible. In fact, it wasn't until the passage in 1974 of the Equal Credit Opportunity Act that women won the legal right to apply for credit cards without their husbands.

Credit cards as we know them today grew from the Diners Club card in 1950, where the cardholder had to pay the entire balance each month, to introducing magnetic stripe verification in the 1960s, and smart chip technology introduced to US consumers in October 2015. Now, well into the twenty-first century, we have a "buy now, pay later" culture that is commonly accepted. Despite complaints about credit bureau overreach and reporting errors, our current system is far less discriminatory than ever. That doesn't mean it's perfect; it's far from it.

## Competition Brings Change

Several years ago, the three main credit bureaus created VantageScore in order to compete in the market in search of greater profit. The main credit score, used by over 90% of lenders, is called the FICO score. FICO, a data analytics company, got its name from the business's founders, Bill Fair and Earl Isaac, in 1956. The company focuses mainly on consumer credit risk and sells the three-digit classic score, which ranges from 300 to 850.

Besides the base credit score, there are additional scores like FICO Auto Scores used in mortgage lending, and FICO Bankcard Scores. These versions range from 250 to 900. Many lenders use the information on a credit report and also employ their proprietary scoring model. They may even give a letter grade such as A, B, or C rather than a number. The type of loan you are seeking will influence the risk assessment as well. For instance, a mortgage lender will look at all three big credit bureaus, Experian, Equifax, and TransUnion, and calculate the average score.

You may have experienced some level of confusion with credit reporting and scoring. In fact, past reporters have spent years on assignment striving for a "perfect" score only to fall short. According to the Fair Issac Corporation, less than 2% of the population actually gets 850, the highest FICO score possible.[127]

I've reviewed tens of thousands of credit reports and scores, and I've never seen an 850. While I have seen scores in the high 820s to the 830s, after a certain point, the exact number doesn't matter. Here's a rough breakdown of how lenders view various groupings of FICO Scores:

- Exceptional 800+

- Very good 740 to 799

- Good 670 to 739

- Fair 580 to 669

- Poor 579 and lower[128]

Most lenders consider a FICO base score above 760 an excellent score. They will probably approve a loan application if we satisfy the lender with other factors like income and debt ratio. Everything being equal, we're not likely to receive better terms on a loan if we have a 770 vs. 820 score. However, there is an actual cost between the highest and lowest tiers. Consider the difference in cost on a thirty-year, $400,000 mortgage with an APR of 4% vs. 8%. The difference is $369,143 extra in interest paid to the lender over thirty years.

Income doesn't affect the score. I've seen very low-income households with credit scores above 800 and have also seen plenty of six-figure earners with scores in the low 600s. While

FICO doesn't release the exact details of their "secret sauce," they provide an overview of the factors affecting every score.

## Calculating the Score

Let's break each section down starting with the most significant factor, **payment history**, which accounts for 35%, more than one-third of the score. This concept is straightforward; on-time payments are good, and late payments impact the score negatively. The nuance in this section lies with recency and severity.

The most recent payment history has greater weight in the scoring model. You could have years of on-time payments, but a few recent late payments will lower your score. This gets into the severity portion. The greater the number of late payments on one account, and/or the greater the number of accounts reported as late, the more severe the impact will be on the score. Accounts become reported to the credit bureaus as late when the payment is over thirty days late.

The **amounts owed** section accounts for 30% of the score. This portion considers account balances but also credit utilization, which is the term for the amount of money owed relative to the available credit. This applies to revolving debt such as credit cards. For instance, a $1,000 balance on an account with a $1,000 limit would mean 100% utilization. A $500 balance and a $1,000 limit would mean 50% utilization.

Though it may be counterintuitive, using an account can lower your credit score. The higher the utilization is, the greater the negative impact will be. A general rule is to keep your utilization below 20% of your credit limit. If you spend over 20% of your limit, then your credit score will drop.

For instance, if you have a credit limit of $5,000, it's best to keep the balance under $1,000. Beware. You can still have a high reported amount owed, even if you pay your card balances in full every month. Credit card companies report each account to credit bureaus on different dates, and those dates differ from your billing cycle. The statement cycle affects the payment due date, but is independent of credit reporting.

Consider a credit card account with a payment due on the tenth of each month, and the credit card company reports balances to the credit bureau on the first of every month. If you pay your balance in full after the first, there will still be a balance on the credit report. Individual account utilization and cumulative usage, or the total amount owed relative to the combined available credit, can affect your credit.

Depending on your situation, hearing the oversimplified advice to pay all bills on time and keep revolving balances low may be frustrating. It may not even be possible at the moment. If that is the case, I encourage you to seek help. There are many helpful counselors and coaches who can help you get your debt under control.

Credit cards can be a great tool and may offer fantastic rewards. Paying the balances in full every month will help you ensure you don't let your debts get out of control and that you avoid paying interest. Even if this goal seems out of reach, it's still worthwhile to strive toward. If you're using a high percentage of credit, lenders may think that you're overextended and that you may be a greater risk for defaulting.

**Length of credit history** is the next largest section of the FICO score, which accounts for 15%. I think of this section as building trust with action. As a general rule, a longer history will help increase your score. Your FICO scores take these measures into account:

- How long your credit accounts have been open, including the age of your oldest account, the age of your newest account, and an average age of all your accounts

- How long it has been since you used accounts

The last two sections have equal weight in the calculation of the FICO score: **types of credit in use** and **new credit** account for 10% each of the total score. The credit mix includes credit cards, retail accounts, installment loans, finance company accounts, and mortgage loans. It doesn't mean that you need every type of account to have an excellent score. Remember to keep each section in perspective. This section is a small portion of the overall score.

The last part, new credit, comes into play every time you apply for a new account. Even if you're denied a loan, each time you apply, it counts as a "hard" inquiry and lowers your score. The more recent the inquiries, the lower your score will be.

There are some exceptions to the rule. Shopping for mortgages is the most notable. When looking for the best home loan, consumers have a forty-five-day window where all mortgage inquiries only count as one. As a general rule, only apply for credit when you need it. Anyone can check their credit score as often as they'd like without negative impact. These "soft" inquiries do not affect your credit score. As a general rule, only apply for credit when you need it. Anyone can check their credit score as often as they'd like without negative impact. These "soft" inquiries do not affect your credit score. and no one else can see these inquiries. Beware, when we apply for a loan, the hard inquiry activates "credit triggers" or "trigger leads". Credit bureaus sell the leads to lenders and insurance companies who are looking for pre-screened customers. You can opt out of receiving these solicitations by calling toll-free **1-888-5-OPTOUT (1-888-567-8688)** or visiting http://www .optoutprescreen.com.

## United, but Different

While the details of scores matter, it's crucial to not lose sight of the big picture. I'd like to offer my own personal examples. Before my wife and I married over fifteen years ago, we sat down and discussed our finances. We printed credit reports, shared financial statements, and brought our individual budgets to the table. We left no stone unturned. Our goal was to understand each other's habits and work toward one unified plan.

Our families had different values in raising us as children, and it affected how we treated money. My wife grew up in Massachusetts, though she was born in Hong Kong. Her family had some traditional Chinese values and experiences, which influenced their parenting. As a child, my mother-in-law walked to the well and had to carry buckets of water to the house for the water supply. My father-in-law had many siblings, and food was scarce. He's told me stories of how he had to get to the dinner table quickly and eat as fast as possible or the food would be gone.

My wife's parents taught her frugality and exemplified it in their lives. When they moved to the US, they had very little and relied on the generosity and family values of my mother-in-law's parents, who had a house in the Boston suburbs. My wife's grandmother had fled mainland China to Hong Kong during WWII with a child on her back and the items she could carry. With fierce determination, she married, saved money, and made a life full of opportunity for her children and grandchildren.

My in-laws made the most of the opportunity, gained skills for productive careers, and saved for the things they considered necessary. Family stability and a solid future for their children topped the list. After living with family members, they purchased a modest home with mostly cash and saved for their children's education. Their determination and foresight provided college opportunities for their children.

My wife was fortunate to graduate from a prestigious school with very little student loan debt. Her parents taught her that if you want to buy something, you save for it. When she needed a car to drive to work, she bought it with cash, understanding that taking on debt would drag her down. She had little knowledge about the specific details of credit scoring, but she understood solid financial principles and stayed the course.

My upbringing was different. I was born and raised in New England during a time of growing consumerism. My parents gave me and my brothers everything they could buy to make us happy. They lived above their means, and the success of my grandfather subsidized our lives. We had lots of stuff. Christmas and birthdays were lavish. We came to expect the next new thing.

My son makes fun of me now because he's seen the VHS tapes of the celebrations and one particular moment when I received my first pocket knife. I screamed with glee. Pinching pennies and planning for the distant future weren't values I learned. I learned frugality through scarcity when I moved out of my parents' home at age sixteen. There were days when I didn't have food and lacked transportation to get to a grocery store, which was over thirty miles away.

Through grace and serendipity, I survived and built a career. A friend suggested that because I was a high school dropout, a GED would be beneficial for my future, so I took the test. Some other friends suggested college, but I lacked the funds and feared the price tag and student debt.

I had friends who supported me and my life took many more twists and turns that may make it into some future book, but for now, I'm presenting the simplified version. I'd be remiss in omitting my gratitude to Howard, Gary, Steve, Cire, Tim, and the many others who helped keep me alive and growing as a young adult.

The credit counseling industry was a learning experience for me. I learned the nuances of credit scoring. Though, as we're aware, knowledge doesn't automatically lead to success. I had the "buy now, pay later" mentality and simply felt better by buying stuff. Sometimes I justified personal wants as needs. Living on the third floor, I "needed" an air conditioner, so I bought a fancy programmable one that made the room ice-cold on a timer. This way I could come home and relax. My spending mentality led to credit card debt.

When my wife and I sat down to review our finances, I owed about $8,000. This may or may not sound like a lot to you; however, with my $20,000 salary, it was a significant amount. Despite the debt, I prided myself on the fact that the payments were current and my credit score was excellent.

I understood how to work the credit system and found comfort in the arbitrary benchmark. The fact is that I had habits that, without change, would have led to financial catastrophe. My wife, without knowledge of what went into a credit score, had an excellent score too. She lived a disciplined life and only bought what she needed and paid her bills in full every month. She didn't have any debt, and she had developed habits that served her well. Financial health was her personal goal, and she was in tip-top shape.

It took considerable work to bring our different philosophies, habits, and personalities into one workable plan. Remember cassette tapes and CDs? My wife alphabetized her music, while mine didn't always match the corresponding cases. This is one minor example of how very different we are. Despite the differences, we continue to make it work.

First, we started with a common foundation. For us as Christians, the Bible provided core guiding principles in many areas of our life together, including how we manage money. Love may sound cheesy, but in our lives, it was an active verb. When we remember that love always protects, it informs our decisions and creates stability. We were honest and open about finances. We chose to trust each other. Through all difficulties, sicknesses and health, rich and poor times, we persevered. Love never failed us as we were getting started in our relationship, and it still guides us now almost twenty years later.

Communication continues to be a fundamental part of our success. Both of our credit scores have been above 800 throughout our marriage. This isn't because we've obsessed over the details. We focused on making the best decisions possible while building our life together. That doesn't mean that it was easy. We've persevered through job loss, deaths of loved ones, challenges of adoption, and life-threatening disease.

With a focus on overall well-being, you'll be less likely to get stressed with details that may have little bearing on your financial situation. Sometimes what's best for the credit score is not best for the individual. For instance, sometimes opening new credit card accounts could increase your score by lowering the total utilization. For some people, the additional available credit is too tempting and results in additional debt.

Groups like Debtors Anonymous and Spenders Anonymous exist for a good reason. Advertisers understand the addictive allure of the "buy now, pay later" mentality. The idea of "retail therapy" has made it into households across the income spectrum. Too often, I've heard, "There are more bills than I can afford, so I'm going shopping because it makes me feel better." With interest rates of 25 to 30%, retail credit cards are often an expensive endeavor.

For some people, access to borrowing is a dangerous trap. For others, it's leverage to purchase wealth-building assets. The question for each of us is, "How will I use credit?"

The danger for us as consumers is to believe that our credit score, a three-digit financial risk assessment, means more than it does. It is not a judgment about personal values or moral character. A credit score only reflects how we've managed debt and finances in the past. Though we can't change what's already occurred, we can take steps today to build a different future. The first step is easy and free. Get your credit report.

Yes, credit is important. Never forget that it's financial well-being and whole health wealth that we're building. This is a lifelong process and not a destination quantified by a single number.

# MONEY TALK Q&A

## Q: Will credit scoring change over time?

A: Yes, the current model of credit reporting and scoring will continue to change. Some legislators would like to move credit reports out of the hands of the three bureaus and into the hands of the Consumer Financial Protection Bureau (CFPB). The new government agency would accept nontraditional payment histories such as rent and utility bill payments, which are currently neutral-negative. Neutral in the sense that the payments aren't generally reported when they're made on time. Negative, since they appear when the accounts are past due, often when they're sent to collection agencies, as I mentioned earlier.

FICO has over ten different scoring models and versions of their score. VantageScore has also had multiple iterations. The first two ranged from 501 to 990. The latest versions, 3.0 and 4.0, use the same range as the FICO base score, 300 to 850.

## Q: Should I close a credit card that I paid off?

A: It depends. Here are some factors to consider. Utilization affects a significant portion of your credit score. Before closing an account, weigh the impact the action will have on your ratio of overall balance to available credit.

Closing a revolving account will have a different impact on different people. For instance, imagine two people both closing an account with a $500 limit. One person has $50,000 remaining available credit on other accounts, and the other person only has $500 remaining. The person with the smaller limit will have a much higher utilization when they charge purchases in the future, which will lower their credit score.

Consider how long the account has been open. A longer credit history will always have a positive effect on your FICO score; the length of history accounts for 15% of the score. Consider as well how many revolving accounts you have. If you close the only account you have, you'll reduce the mix of credit, which comprises 10% of the score.

## Q: Should I pay bills early to keep utilization low?

A: Remember that utilization only matters with revolving accounts. Paying a utility bill early won't affect your credit score. If you pay a revolving account such as a credit card too early, it may not post to your credit report. Some people call to make a payment soon after they charge something on the account. You won't build credit if they don't report the balance to the credit bureaus. In fact, you might end up "not scored" or you may have a "thin file" due to lack of activity in your report.

## Q: What if creditors harass me at work?

A: It's not necessarily illegal for a debt collector to contact you at work. The Fair Debt Collection Practices Act prohibits the calls if the collector "has reason to know" that your employer prohibits those calls (15 USC § 1692c). For more legal advice and information, check out Nolo: www.nolo.com/legal-encyclopedia /can-creditor-me-work-collect-debt.html.

## Q: Can creditors send me to jail?

A: No. However, there's a *but*. Congress outlawed debtors' prisons in 1833. However, committing fraud or willfully choosing not to pay a fine or fee can result in jailing. Failure to pay child support can result in jail time. If you ever receive a court summons for any debt, DO NOT IGNORE IT. Get legal help if you can afford it. If there is truly no way you can pay your debt, you can ask the court to dismiss the debt. Make sure you have a good reason, like identity theft, horrible service, or the statute of limitations expired. The legal system can be scary, but it's not all bad.

For more information about credit scores, including a free booklet on understanding FICO scoring, visit www.MattParadise.com/capablebonus.

# 16

## IT'S NOT FAKE NEWS

### Scams, Fraud, and ID Theft

E very state has a workforce agency. Massachusetts branded the employment and training resource centers as MassHire, which serve the community. MassHire creates and sustains powerful connections between businesses and job seekers through a statewide network of employment professionals. They train the employees to assist everyone who walks through their doors with tools and resources to further their careers. This background information is important, because, as you might imagine, employees of the agency receive extensive training and have greater consumer safety awareness than the average person.

One MassHire employee, Eddie, came to me for some counseling as he was in the middle of an epic battle with his bank. He explained to me how someone had fraudulently used his debit card. He was traveling to another state for a family emergency. A relative passed away, and the family needed Eddie to help with funeral arrangements.

While on the trip, he went to a restaurant and paid with his debit card. After spending a couple of months with his family, he came home to Massachusetts to discover that someone had used his card to charge more than $18,000. There were furniture purchases, food expenses, and more. Some research concluded that a server at the restaurant where he had dined out of state on his family trip had "skimmed" the account information from his card and had used it to go on some wild shopping sprees.

Eddie felt violated. It embarrassed him to ask for my help because, as he said, "I should have known better."

One of the first things he asked was, "Can't the police help?"

The answer to that valuable question comes from a former con man, Frank Abagnale Jr.

"The police can't protect consumers. People need to be more aware and educated about identity theft. You need to be a little bit wiser, a little bit smarter and there's nothing wrong with being skeptical. We live in a time when, if you make it easy for someone to steal from you, someone will."

His book, *Catch Me If You Can*[129], inspired the blockbuster hit about Abagnale and his life as a professional fraudster.

Identity theft occurs when someone uses your identifying information, such as your name, social security number, or credit card number without your permission to commit fraud or other crimes. According to TransUnion, 33% of US adults have experienced identity theft, which is more than twice the global average.[130]

Thieves use many ways to get your personal information. They can open credit cards or take out loans in your name or access existing accounts and make purchases. They can drain your bank accounts, open utility accounts, file fraudulent tax returns, get employment, use medical services, and even accumulate criminal violations in your name.

I taught a workshop where one participant shared his personal experience with ID theft. He was traveling for business to a state he had never visited in his life. While driving, police pulled him over for a minor traffic violation. Much to his surprise, the officer asked him to step out of the car and then arrested him for outstanding warrants.

Apparently, someone had gotten his personal identification and used it while committing crimes. Everything was eventually sorted out, but the identity theft came at an actual cost. The man missed meetings and, not least of all, endured major emotional stress.

Another story comes from an individual at an emergency homeless shelter. I was teaching about the importance of credit reporting, since it's often a significant barrier to employment and stable, safe housing. As part of the sessions, I accessed and reviewed reports with everyone who was interested.

John was in complete shock when we found more than $80,000 of outstanding debt in his name. As we researched the situation, we determined that his brother had stolen social security numbers of family members and had accumulated significant debts, including car loans, leased furniture, and credit card charges. The brother had passed away six months earlier, which complicated the resolution.

Unfortunately, fixing the theft takes time and patience, even when the circumstances of homelessness require urgency. The costs of identity theft are staggering. According to the Javelin Strategy & Research Identity 2022 Fraud Study, identity fraud resulted in $52 billion of loss affecting 42 million US victims.[131]

In the time it took me to write this chapter, identity thieves stole millions of dollars. Educating yourself about the topic will help lower your risk of becoming a victim.

When protecting ourselves, I use the analogy of driving or riding in a vehicle. Research has shown that wearing seatbelts saves lives. Seatbelts reduce the risk of death by 45% and cut the risk of serious injury by 50%. Seatbelts save thousands of lives each year, but millions of people choose not to use them.[132]

Tragically, auto accidents still occur. As long as auto transportation exists, it's impossible to eliminate the risk of related injury. However, we can take many steps every time we get into a car to lower risk and minimize injury. Besides wearing your seatbelt, avoid driving while tired, never drive under the influence, stay calm, never use a cell phone while driving, obey speed limits and posted signs, and more.

As an adult, I find it easy to be overconfident in my driving safety. The steps listed above are, after all, basic common sense, right? It's all too easy to drive when I'm tired, to let emotions get the best of me when someone cuts me off in traffic, or to get distracted while I'm driving. If you've ever driven with a child in the car, particularly a young child, you know it's almost impossible to not get distracted at some point.

By now, you're wondering what driving has to do with ID theft. Living in the modern world comes with inherent risk. Just like the only way to eliminate auto-related risks is to avoid vehicles altogether, the only way to get rid of the risk of fraud is to sever our associations with civilization. If you're reading this book, that's not the path you chose. You can take some common-sense steps to reduce your risks. The first step to avoid identity theft is to familiarize yourself with the ways identity theft and fraud occur.

## How Thieves Target You

A popular way thieves get information is by "skimming." Thieves often use a device called a skimmer installed at gas pumps or ATMs to collect card data. Small enough to carry while concealed, the device can also be handheld.

I worked with a security expert in Boston to find out how much personal information was on an old ATM, the kind you've probably seen in many convenience stores, shopping malls, and gas stations.

> FYI, I suggest that you never use these small semi-portable automated tellers. Not only are they less secure, they also charge a fee for convenience. ATM fees can stack up quickly. This security expert purchased a machine on eBay for a few hundred dollars and worked with a tech-savvy friend to print hundreds of feet of account data from the machine.

Technology such as skimmers will continue to develop, and in a digital world, thieves adapt. However, new sophisticated tech isn't the only way to get data. Even though theft of paper mail carries penalties and jail time, we send lots of personal identification through the post office. Mail carriers deliver documents such as social security cards, birth certificates, driver's licenses, photo identification, new checks, tax information, preapproval offers, credit cards, and account information of all types. Thieves can grab the material right from a mailbox.

It's our responsibility to always keep an eye out for expected mail. For instance, they deliver your credit card statement around the same time every month. If the date comes and goes without delivery, investigate it. Even if the company made a mistake and didn't mail the statement, if there was a delay, or if they lost the statement in transit, you, as the consumer, are still responsible for on-time payments.

Many people throw away all kinds of sensitive information, like bills, statements, and documents. Thieves are aware of this and can search your trash or recycling bins to find a treasure trove of information. I recommend using a cross-cut shredder that turns sensitive account data and personal information into confetti.

Your trash or the mail are the only place thieves can find personal information. Consider what's in your car, purse, or wallet. I've had the benefit of participating in identity theft workshops with credit bureaus, local police, and the FBI. Before my trainings and certifications, I was clueless. My logic was that if I carried all documents with me at all times, they were safer than in any other location. My wallet held my credit cards, my driver's license, my social security card, my birth certificate, and more.

As you might imagine, I experienced significant stress when I misplaced the precious cargo. It combined my wallet with a PalmPilot case. PalmPilots were devices eventually made obsolete by cell phones. I laugh as I write this because the technology seemed innovative.

Because the case was so large, I placed it on the roof of my car while pumping gas one day. It was cold out, snowing, and being in a hurry, I finished pumping gas and drove off. As soon as I remembered my wallet, I drove back and searched along the route. The street was busy and covered in snow, and in despair, I gave up the search and headed home.

Much to my surprise, a kind stranger found everything and returned it using the address on my license. I was grateful to have all the documents back. Unfortunately, the PalmPilot device was crushed while lying in the street. In short, don't be like me and risk losing valuable information by carrying it with you everywhere.

Pretexting is another way criminals may get personal information. This is where thieves use false pretenses to get your info. You've likely received some scam phone calls. Many unsuspecting victims give out personal identification numbers (PINs), account information, and other data over the phone before realizing their mistake.

"Phishing" is the fraudulent practice of sending emails while pretending to be representing reputable companies in order to induce individuals to reveal personal information. Variations on the theme include spear phishing, vishing, SMiShing, and pharming.

- Spear phishing involves prior research on individuals and targets them specifically.

- Unlike targeted email phishing, vishing involves the phone and is the combination of two words, *voice* and *phishing*. This fraudulent practice of making calls or leaving voicemails to get information ensnares people who are less tech-savvy, especially the elderly.

- SMiShing uses text messages to trick you into giving out your private information.

- Pharming is a scamming practice where hackers install malicious code on a personal computer (PC) or server, misdirecting users to fraudulent websites. The purpose of the fake site is to steal usernames, passwords, financial data, and other personal information.

Electronic scams and fraud occur every day. The more we're educated about how they happen, the less likely we'll become a victim. Malware is a catchall term used by computer professionals to mean a variety of forms of hostile, intrusive, or annoying software or program code. Common types of malware include viruses, keyloggers, worms, trojans, ransomware/crypto-malware, logic bombs, bots/botnets, adware, spyware, and rootkits.

Technology changes rapidly. One resource that will help you remain educated is the Cybersecurity and Infrastructure Security Agency (www.cisa.gov).

As technology advances, the list of fraudulent practices will change. The FBI publishes a list of the most common scams, crimes, and tips to avoid becoming a victim. You can find the most up-to-date information here: https://www.fbi.gov/scams-and-safety.

## Prevention Is Key

It's scary to consider the many ways thieves can victimize us. The more educated and aware we are, the more we can reduce the risk. Much like fear of car accidents, fear of scams or theft can paralyze us during critical moments. Life moves quickly and we need to stay alert. Consider implementing some simple but effective suggestions like these:

- Update virus protection regularly on any computer that accesses the internet. You can review pros and cons of various antivirus software from sources such as *PCMag*, CNET, Tom's Guide, and *Consumer Reports*. Fun fact: many libraries offer free access to *Consumer Reports*. My library has printed copies available, but they also provide online access.

- Only purchase items on a secured and trusted internet site. A secure URL should begin with https.

- Consider using credit cards over debit cards for the additional protections credit cards offer. Personally, I rarely buy anything online with my debit card.

- If there is fraudulent activity on your account, remember that reporting the fraud early is key to minimizing the loss. The Electronic Fund Transfer Act provides some protection, but it's not 100%. When you report within two business days of discovery, it limits your losses to $50. If you report sixty days after the unauthorized transaction appears on your statement, you could lose up to $500 of what the thief withdraws. If you wait over sixty days, you could lose all the money that was taken from your account.

- Regularly review all monthly statements and reconcile every charge for credit and debit cards. Sometimes thieves will charge a small amount to see if the account is active and may follow up with a much larger amount next time. Don't ignore unrecognized small amounts on your bill.

- Place difficult-to-guess passwords/PINs on your accounts and physical devices, such as your phone and computer. Passwords can be frustrating. Some people choose password managers to make it easier to handle a variety of accounts. There are pros and cons to the practice. While it may be more convenient to store all passwords in one place, if the password manager software gets hacked, a thief may have an easier time accessing all of your account information.

- While I'm on the subject of computers and phones, only download software and apps from trusted sources, and make sure your operating systems and apps are always up-to-date. I set them to auto-update, since I sometimes forget to check if I have the latest version or not. Many of the updates provide security fixes and minimize vulnerabilities.

- Minimize the use of public Wi-Fi and, if you use it, be wary of the sites, passwords, and transactions on your device. It's relatively easy for a thief to capture sensitive communication at the vast majority of public hotspots—locations such as cafés, restaurants, airports, and hotels. On a public network, someone else may access your emails, passwords, and unencrypted instant messages.

- Don't carry PINs or passwords around, and avoid bringing unnecessary documents with you. As I shared earlier, it's easy to lose a wallet. Learn from my mistake and leave critical documents in a secure location. My mother recently had her purse stolen. It only took a moment in a parking lot. She was bringing her groceries from the store to her car. In the blink of an eye, when she carried a bag from the shopping cart to her trunk, someone snatched her purse. By the time she noticed, the thief was gone. On any day, backpacks and belongings are strewn across floors of college campuses and libraries. Always keep your personal effects secure.

- Only give your social security number (SSN) when necessary. If someone asks for your SSN, ask: Why do you need my SSN? How will you use my SSN? How do you protect my SSN from being misused? What will happen if I don't give my SSN?

- Ask about information security at work, businesses, doctors' offices, and elsewhere. I received the standard new patient package when I visited a new doctor. The office asked for personal information so they could contact me, bill insurance, and keep accurate medical records. One item they asked for was my SSN. I politely asked if it was necessary to write the number on the form and was told, "No, it's just a standard form and we don't need it." While I need some level of trust with my care providers, if they don't require extra personal information, I prefer to minimize the risk of it being stolen.

- Carefully review all paperwork, such as your Explanation of Benefits and bills, and shred, shred, shred. While this list of tips isn't exhaustive, it gives you some practical ideas to safeguard your personal information and lower the risk of becoming a victim of a scam or identity theft.

## If You Become a Victim

I've discussed some prevention tips. Let's talk about what we can do if you become a victim.

While the entire process takes time, take these steps. First, contact the companies that you know were involved in the fraud or scam. Many companies have a special department to handle fraud and can help you with the process. Ask them to close or freeze all affected accounts. That way, they need your approval for additional charges.

If credit cards or bank cards were affected, companies will often issue new cards quickly. Change log-ins, passwords, and personal identification numbers (PINs) for your accounts. After contacting the companies directly, place a fraud alert on your credit reports. Place a free, one-year fraud alert by contacting one of three credit bureaus. That company must tell the other two.

- Experian (www.experian.com/help),
  (888) EXPERIAN or (888) 397-3742

- TransUnion (www.transunion.com/credit-help),
  (888) 909-8872

- Equifax (www.equifax.com/personal/credit-report-services), (800) 685-1111

The fraud alert will make it harder for someone to open new accounts in your name. When you have an alert on your report, a business must verify your identity before it issues new credit in your name. You can renew the fraud alert after one year. Keep an eye out for correspondence. You'll receive a letter from each credit bureau, which will confirm that they placed a fraud alert on your file.

You can also freeze your credit for free. This will prevent access to your report and will prevent someone from getting new credit in your name. Even with a freeze, some companies, such as employers, insurance agencies, and the government, can still access your reports. Remember, you need to lift the freeze before you apply for any new accounts, including a credit card, a personal loan, a new mortgage, or a refinance. Consumers need to be at least eighteen years old to place a freeze online, but parents, legal guardians, or others with power of attorney can place a security freeze on credit reports of minors under the age of sixteen. Minors, sixteen or seventeen years old, may request their own security freeze by phone or mail.

When reviewing your reports, make a note of any account or transaction you don't recognize. This will help you report the theft to the Federal Trade Commission (FTC) and the police. The FTC is a consumer advocate agency that assists with identity theft. If you become a victim, you can report the theft to them (www.identitytheft.gov). Complete their online form or call (877) 438-4338. Include as many details as possible. Based on the information you enter, you'll receive your identity theft report and recovery plan.

Your identity theft report helps when following up with businesses about the identity theft. It also guarantees you certain rights. If you create an account with the FTC, they'll walk you through each recovery step, track your progress, and pre-fill forms and letters for you. If you don't create an account, you must print and save your identity theft report and recovery plan right away. Once you leave the page on their website, you won't be able to access or update them.

I recommend filing a fraud claim with your local police department. Bring a copy of your FTC identity theft report along with a government-issued photo ID, proof of your address (for example, mortgage statement, rental agreement, or utility bill), and any other proof you have of the theft (such as bills or IRS notices).

Tell the police someone stole your identity and you need to file a report. Be sure to ask for a copy of the police report. You may need this to follow up with fraudulent accounts. I've helped clients through this process. Many of them had utility fraud, where someone opened unauthorized accounts in their name.

Unfortunately, I have seen hundreds of cases where parents opened an account for electricity in their child's name. Many years later, the child became an adult and needed an apartment but found delinquent accounts preventing them from getting a place of their own. It is a difficult and emotional decision for someone to consider filing a police report on their parents. In my experience, utility companies require a police report to resolve cases of fraud.

Few landlords will rent apartments to someone who isn't able to turn on the electricity. Before you judge, poverty comes with many challenges. It confronts loving parents with complicated dilemmas. While I'm not condoning placing utilities in children's names, please understand that multigenerational poverty has many layers of complexity. It's a tough choice to remain homeless or not to have electrical service, or to place utilities in a child's name.

Take a deep breath. Even writing about identity theft raises my pulse. It's stressful to consider. As you work through the process, know that you're not alone. As you take one intentional step after another, be confident that you're building whole health wealth.

# MONEY TALK Q&A

## Q: Where can I get help with my consumer rights?

A: You can find state and federal consumer protection offices and agencies here:

- www.usa.gov/state-consumer

- www.consumerfinance.gov/

- www.nolo.com/legal-encyclopedia/consumer -protection

- www.justice.gov/civil/consumer-information

- www.nclc.org/

## Q: Is ID theft services/insurance worth the cost?

A: If you're considering a service to protect you, make sure you research the details and weigh the pros and cons. You can consider resources like *Consumer Reports* for advice. Some of their articles claim that do-it-yourself strategies are just as effective as paid services.

## Q: Should I lock or freeze my credit report?

A: If you've been a victim of ID theft, it's worth seriously considering. A credit lock may cost a fee for the service. As of 2022, a federal law, the Economic Growth, Regulatory Relief, and Consumer Protection Act, requires free credit freezing and unfreezing. While freezes make it much more difficult for anyone to access your report, they aren't foolproof. It's still important to monitor your reports. Also, consider when you may need credit. If you need to open a new account or refinance your mortgage, there will be additional steps to gain legitimate access to your report.

If you'd like a free forty-page guide on identity theft, a College Student's Guide to Fraud, and Scams, Schemes, and Swindles, go to www.MattParadise.com/capablebonus.

# 17

# DON'T LEAVE SHORE WITHOUT A FINANCIAL LIFE PRESERVER

Leaving the house can be dangerous. Car accidents happen every day. It doesn't mean we should never go out, but it is wise to wear seatbelts and follow safety recommendations. Risk is part of life. Managing risk helps to lower your stress and protect your assets. Whether you are investing for your retirement or for more immediate needs, there are three major things that can keep you from achieving your financial goals: inflation, taxes, and risk.

It's one thing to plan for inflation and to minimize the taxes you owe, but risk is another matter because the future is so unpredictable. Financial risks can come in many forms, but the results are always the same: loss of money—possibly because of loss of family income from death, disability, illness, legal action, or other circumstances beyond your control.

Sometimes the loss is trivial, while at other times it may cause significant hardship. There is no way to eliminate all risks, but there are ways to avoid them, minimize them, or protect yourself and your family from them. When a risk is too costly to assume, you need ways to manage it. Insurance provides a convenient way to manage financial loss caused by catastrophic risk.

You can manage risk in four ways: assume risk, avoid risk, share risk, and transfer risk to someone else.

When you **assume risk**, you do nothing to minimize the impact of loss should a hazard occur. Let's say you don't buy fire or flood insurance on your home or you don't have life, disability, or health insurance coverage. Should an unfavorable event occur, you must pay the full cost of the loss out of your own assets.

**Avoiding risk** may not be easy, but there are ways to lower risk management expenses by doing so. Risk avoidance can lower the cost of risk, which is why insurance premiums are lower for people and businesses that take precautionary measures to lower risk.

For example, automobile insurance premiums are lower for drivers with good driving records (meaning no accidents and no cited violations of driving laws), and nonsmokers pay lower medical insurance and life insurance premiums than smokers do.

Doing nothing is not a strategy to avoid risk. Inflation will whittle away your wealth by decreasing the purchasing power if you choose to bury your money in a hole or put it under the mattress.

We all regularly **share risk**. When we pay taxes, they pool together our dollars with money from other taxpayers to pay for police, fire, and military protection. Personal insurance usually requires risk-sharing as deductibles and premiums. You take on the responsibility for a small portion of risk, while transferring the larger part of risk to the insurer.

Insurance is a popular way to **transfer risk**. Mortgage companies require homeowners to purchase adequate insurance coverage while repaying a loan. We transfer the risk of lost income for our loved ones with life insurance. We transfer the risk of huge monetary loss from a vehicular accident with auto insurance. People can also transfer risk to other individuals with a legal contract.

Businesses often transfer risk through an indemnification clause. You've likely transferred risk by signing an agreement to hold an entity harmless; for example, when you or your children took part in sports, went on adventure courses, used eBay, rode in an Uber, consumed NPR media, used a cell phone—you get the point. The list goes on and on.

## May I Repeat Myself? Keep It Personal

The details of how you choose to manage risk are personal. We all have different circumstances and should plan accordingly. For instance, life insurance isn't for everyone; I don't believe that a policy for children is appropriate. Many people benefit from a term life policy to help provide security for their loved ones in the event of their untimely death.

Some wealthy people buy life insurance to cover the taxes their estates incur. Estates can avoid taxes when they hold assets in a trust. For most people, this isn't a concern because it only applies to estates worth more than $11 million for individuals and double that for married couples. The government complicates tax law and changes it frequently. For the most current regulations, consult with a tax professional.

As a general rule, I steer clients away from buying life insurance on children. They often sell the products using fear-based strategies, such as paying for children's funerals or education. Whole life insurance policies are usually expensive for what you get. Most people are better off keeping life insurance separate from investing. There are most often less expensive and more beneficial strategies and products such as a 529 for education and a 401(k), IRA, or other accounts for retirement.

If you have children, a spouse, or other family members who rely on your income, life insurance can provide some security and peace of mind. If your goal is to build wealth separately and eventually not need a policy, then term life is your best bet.

Buying insurance is less expensive when you're young and healthy. After all, the company is betting their business that they won't have to pay. An underwriter is an insurance company employee who will evaluate the risk of insuring you. They want to know every part of your life. More than just your current health status, they're interested in potential risk factors. Here are a few factors that can raise your life insurance premium:

- **Age** – the older you are, the more you pay

- **Gender** – women generally pay lower rates than men

- **Driving experience/record** – insurers often consider your last five years of driving history

- **Tobacco use** – smoking, dipping, or vaping increases rates

- **Hobbies** – high-risk activities like rock-climbing or motorcycle-riding increase cost

- **Occupation** – some risky jobs like police or firefighter can lead to denied insurance coverage

- **Physical condition** – insurers consider dozens of risk factors for illness

- **Body Mass Index (BMI)** – too high or too low is risky

- **Current or past drug use** – Companies offering standard term or permanent life insurance can refuse to cover you

Life insurance companies want to know everything about you, and if you try to "bend the truth," they can deny a future claim. Providing false information during your insurance application is called material misrepresentation

I found getting insurance stressful; however, the research was well worth the $20,000 in savings. With industry insight, I addressed the underwriter, who agreed to cut my annual premium in half.

Before purchasing insurance, make sure you compare rates. Different companies may offer better rates for your specific life situation. In addition to insurers' own websites, there are many brokers and websites to help you compare rates. Here are a couple that don't require personal contact information:

- www.policygenius.com/
- www.quotacy.com/

## Types of Life Insurance

It's good to research any product before you make a significant purchase. Life insurance is no different. There are four basic types of life insurance: term life, whole life, universal life, and variable life. Each type has pros and cons.

**Term life insurance** covers you for a preset period, called the policy term. Common periods for coverage are ten, twenty, or thirty years, though there are even one-year terms. Companies will only pay benefits if the insured person dies within that time. After the term expires, the policy has no cash value and won't pay any benefits. This type of life insurance often has the largest benefit (the most money paid to beneficiaries) for the lowest cost.

**Whole life insurance** is a kind of permanent insurance. As long as we pay the premiums, the insurance will stay in effect. Whole life insurance combines a death benefit with a cash-savings feature. The policyholder can borrow against the policy's cash value by taking a policy loan. If you decide to end your policy, the company will pay you the cash value and subtract the amount of any unpaid policy loans and interest.

Insurers market whole life insurance as a good way to save for retirement. Buyer beware—the product has higher commissions and fees than other investments. If you're looking for a tax-advantaged retirement savings, it may make sense to consider other less-expensive investment options. They tie the rate of return on your cash value to the insurer's long-term investment portfolio. Educate yourself thoroughly before buying any product or service to ensure that it will help you accomplish your goals.

**Universal life insurance** offers both permanent insurance protection and a cash value element. With universal life, they place your premium into an investment fund managed by the insurance company. Your cash value earns interest at current market rates. This means that if market interest rates rise, the cash value of your policy will increase, and you may pay lower premiums or skip several premium payments altogether.

If interest rates decline, you may have to pay more than your planned premium to keep the policy. Universal life insurance offers more flexibility than either term life or whole life insurance. Within certain limits, you can increase or decrease the amount of premium payment, increase or decrease the death benefit, and change the frequency of premium payments.

**Variable life insurance** is a kind of permanent insurance that can help to address the adverse effects of inflation on death benefits and cash values. With a variable life insurance policy, they invest your premium payments and your death benefits and cash values vary based on the asset's performance. They will offer you a variety of investment options, such as stock funds, money market funds, or bond funds. Your death benefit amount can go down if the funds lose money. If you decide to cancel the policy, they will pay you the policy's cash value as of the day you cancel.

Unlike whole and universal life insurance, which guarantee a minimum cash value if you surrender your policy, the cash value of a variable life insurance policy may decline to zero. If that happens, you will get nothing back if you cancel the policy. Some variable life insurance policies offer a guaranteed minimum death benefit; however, that feature may cost extra. Be careful: Because of the investment risk, variable life is both an insurance product and a securities contract.

## Too Much Insurance Will Make You Poor

There's no shortage of books and resources about insurance. I won't go into detail about auto insurance, homeowners' insurance, renters' insurance, umbrella policies, pet insurance, or the many other products that you may find useful depending on your particular needs. Insurance possibilities are nearly endless.

Consider these more obscure coverages: wedding insurance and even "cold feet insurance," alien abduction insurance, lotto insurance. (Yes, you read that correctly; if your employees win the lottery, you can purchase insurance to protect against losses stemming from a reduction in productivity and the costs to interview, rehire, or even hire temp workers.) Having children is hard work, and birthing multiple kids can be downright scary. No worries; you can purchase multiple-birth insurance.

Managing risk is paramount. It's critical to consider risk tolerance, set goals, and determine which options are best in your unique situation.

# MONEY TALK Q&A

**Q:** I keep hearing about infinite banking. What is the strategy all about?

**A:** Infinite banking refers to the practice of borrowing money from a dividend paying whole life insurance policy. The concept is that you become your own banker by growing the cash value inside the insurance policy while borrowing against it. You can use the borrowed money for emergencies or other investment opportunities. Some companies also sell Indexed Universal Life Insurance policies for the same purpose.

Infinite banking has its risks. Two of the biggest risks are a reduced death benefit to protect loved ones and the possibility of losing the insurance policy altogether. Policy holders need to keep up with the monthly premiums. Besides those risks, it takes time to build enough cash value to bank on yourself, and other investments can outperform the insurance policy returns. Because of these risks, the strategy is best left to high net worth people.

If you're interested in learning more, consider *Becoming Your Own Banker* by R. Nelson Nash.

To better understand insurance options, including health, auto, home, life, disability, and business insurance, including free access to a 200-page guide to insurance, visit www.MattParadise.com/capablebonus.

# 18

## HOW HEALTHY IS YOUR ESTATE?

Have you ever thought "I don't have enough money" or "I'm too young" to have a long-term financial plan? Consider the fact that 78% of millennials appointed a guardian for their pets during the COVID-19 pandemic. Honestly, I waited until about age thirty-two to have a lawyer draw up a will. Fortunately, nothing bad happened to me before that. Our estate plan brings peace of mind. It would be horrible for Odyssey, our poodle, to end up in a shelter.

Consider how to make sure your assets are taken care of if you own anything of value. Did you know that a study actually showed the return on investment in sets of plastic LEGO blocks can be better than stocks, bonds, and gold? One incredible sale took place in 2017 when a Millennium Falcon set sold for $15,000 at a Las Vegas auction.[133] If you think that sale was impressive, consider that the most expensive Pokémon card blows that price away. In August 2022, a Pikachu Illustrator card sold for $5.275 million![134]

The term *estate* may bring to mind exclusive gated communities for the wealthy. In reality, nearly everyone owns something. Your estate is everything you own or control, including tangible assets, your home and other real estate, vehicles, jewelry, precious metals, coins, collectibles, and personal possessions.

## Wills and Trusts for Loved Ones

Estate planning is about so much more than financial prepara-tion or protection. A will can protect your family from fights, confusion, and the ever-brutal probate court. After a person passes away, probate is the legal procedure by which a court oversees distributing that person's assets. Few people enjoy probate. In fact, my local probate court has a Google rating of 2.1 out of 5 stars.

A will is a legal document that describes our wishes for anything we own of value and minor children (including pets). Only 33% of Americans have created a will, even though it's important. Most people say that they're too busy or don't have enough money to bother.[135]

Do you have pets? No one wants the state to determine the fate of their fur babies. A will can make sure that your pet doesn't end up in an animal shelter. Do you have an important collection? You don't want it sold at a random yard sale.

If you die without a will, the court will appoint a guardian to raise your minor children. Choose a conservator to manage your assets for your dependent children. Require the conserva-tor to post bond and account for every penny spent. Remember: minor children may receive their entire inheritances as early as age eighteen, regardless of their abilities to manage money.

If you don't have the money to pay a lawyer to draft the document, there are resources to help. Nolo provides legal forms, software, books, and e-books (www.nolo.com). Their mission is to help consumers and small businesses find answers to their everyday legal and business questions.

Fun fact: the name of the business comes from the legal phrase *nolo contendere*, which translates to "no contest" or "it will not be disputed" in Latin. The company partnered with the software maker Quicken to provide Nolo's Quicken Will Maker & Trust 2021 for $100. No, I'm not an affiliate and don't earn a commission for a referral. Nolo has been around since the 1970s and is a trusted business, though it's not the only one.

US Legal Wills (www.uslegalwills.com) claims to be America's leading provider of online wills, power of attorney, and living wills. They sell thousands of legal documents every week and have over twenty-one years in business.

Investopedia (www.doyourownwill.com) rates their package a best value. The website has a completely free way to develop a will. No account needed, no credit card, just 100% free with an instant download in Word or PDF format. After some research, determine the best way for you to develop this critical document.

Besides creating a will, consider having a durable power of attorney. This legal document should name the person you want to manage your affairs, show what that person may do on your behalf, and specify the process for determining at what point you cannot manage your own affairs.

Having a healthcare advance directive will allow a person of your choosing to decide for your well-being when you cannot do so. This may also be called a durable power of attorney for healthcare or a proxy. I never imagined that I'd ever need these documents in place—until I did.

My cancer came unexpectedly when I was otherwise healthy and without symptoms. Naming my wife as my healthcare proxy allowed her to make medical decisions during the times I was unconscious and intubated. Another document I'm personally grateful for is the organ donor form. I literally owe my life to the fact someone else, a complete stranger, was an organ donor.

A living trust is a legal document whereby you designate another person, called a trustee, to take responsibility for managing your assets when you're no longer able to.

A living trust allows for the easy transfer of assets while bypassing the often complex and expensive legal process of probate. Living trusts are irrevocable or revocable. Revocable trusts are less expensive, easier to set up, and allow the trustee to make changes. Irrevocable trusts can minimize taxes, help access government benefits, and protect assets from creditors. A downside is that they are less flexible and, unlike revocable trusts, are very difficult to change.

Choosing a trustee is really important. This designee carries a fiduciary responsibility to handle the estate; the trustee has the legal responsibility to manage the trust in the best interest of your chosen beneficiaries.

If you have children, it's crucial to be thoughtful when choosing a trustee. It's also critically important that you have a thoughtful and willing guardian selected. Will the person or family continue to raise your child(ren) with similar values? Will they provide a safe, nurturing environment? If your kid(s) are older, do they know and feel comfortable with the guardian? Is the guardian in the same school district? Do they live far away from family and friends? Is the guardian fiscally responsible? These are just a few of the questions to think about.

My wife and I chose the same person to be the trustee of our estate and the guardian for our son. This would streamline the process to access resources from our trust to ensure they cared for our son and in a timely manner. We sought lots of advice, and the designee discussed our proposition with their family members, including their own children.

In addition to our son, we also care for my wife's parents. They live in our home and we also had to make sure they're taken care of in the event of our untimely demise. Our situation has multiple layers of complexity, and we worked with a lawyer who specializes in walking clients through nuances and complex scenarios.

A living trust can also save money in taxes for heirs. The US tax code is complicated. I will not dig into tax-saving strategies. They are, however, important. A local, compassionate, experienced, and well-qualified certified public accountant (CPA) is your best bet.

It may not be necessary to hire lawyers for smaller estates where probate with a will is an uncontested process. Some assets, like money in a savings account, can go to a beneficiary without probate. Make sure you have named beneficiaries on all accounts. You may not need to establish a trust, but my advice is that everyone should have a will.

As you might imagine, creating an estate plan is emotional, and I suspect that this is a primary reason so many people don't go through the exercise. It's difficult to confront our mortality and consider how our loved ones will continue without us. End-of-life care and discussions about death are challenging. Too often, we avoid hard conversations and family members become passive bystanders. There are many elements besides cost to consider while planning for long-term well-being.

## Caring for the Aging among Us

The COVID-19 pandemic illuminated weaknesses in how we care for elderly and vulnerable. Not only can annual bills run into the hundreds of thousands of dollars, but also many care centers are likely not what you imagine as dignified and fulfilling. An analysis showed that in the forty-three states that reported the data, an astounding 42% of all COVID-19 deaths occurred in nursing homes and assisted living facilities.[136]

In Massachusetts, the average annual cost of nursing home care alone is around $150,000. Private rooms cost even more. Medications and, when necessary, acute care are very expensive. My father-in-law had Medicare and paid for supplemental health insurance, which helps lower the cost of his prescriptions. One of his medications costs $8,000 out of pocket every few weeks.

Medicaid can cover medical costs for those who qualify due to lack of resources. Some families hire attorneys and advisers to help navigate the arduous application process. Each state has different requirements, which adds to the challenge of applying. Many families qualify only after spending all their savings and retirement money.

For some people, long-term care insurance helps, but not everyone can afford it. If we're honest, don't we all desire a rich, fulfilling, and dignified life? Ultimately, we each define what living life to the fullest looks like, but be sure of this: regardless of how it's structured, living life to the fullest requires thoughtful, intentional action.

All this talk about sickness and death is heavy. It's uncomfortable to think about and even more awkward to discuss. One of our most supreme assets is health. You've likely heard the popular saying, "Health is wealth." The more we take care of our bodies, the less we'll have to pay in the long run. I've found this to be true even with an unexpected disease like cancer.

## Health Is Wealth

The factors that contribute to health are called social determinants. The conditions where people live, learn, work, and play affect a wide range of health risks and outcomes.

We group social determinants of health into five areas:

1.  Economic stability

2.  Education access and quality

3.  Healthcare access and quality

4.  Neighborhood and the built environment

5.  Social and community context[137]

You can't just tell people, "Don't be poor; don't live in a poor neighborhood; don't be part of a marginalized group." When it's written in such stark terms, it almost sounds absurd. I've heard many people share similar thoughts about pathways out of poverty: "Some people are just lazy." "Just move to a better place." "Get a better job." "Get more education." Such comments show a general lack of understanding about economic mobility and lack of empathy.

Yes, health is wealth. Wealth is also health. It requires a certain amount of privilege to follow recommendations for optimal health and well-being.

**Move your body**. Active people are less likely to die early.[138]

**Eat well, not too much**. More whole grains, beans, fruits and vegetables, and less meat help avoid disease.[139]

**Reduce stress.** Mental health is critical. Positive thinking increases psychological and physical well-being. Happiness leads to a longer, successful, and fulfilling life.[140]

**Have strong social connections.** Social relationships—both quantity and quality—affect mental health, health behavior, physical health, and mortality risk.[141]

**Have faith.** "Most studies have shown that religious involvement and spirituality are associated with better health outcomes, including greater longevity, coping skills, and health-related quality of life (even during terminal illness) and less anxiety, depression, and suicide. Several studies have shown that addressing the spiritual needs of the patient may enhance recovery from illness."[142]

**Develop purpose.** Dedication to a cause beyond ourselves helps us to get up in the morning, gives our lives meaning and direction, and inspires us to contribute significantly to the world. When we have purpose in our lives, we're more likely to have more optimism, resiliency, and hope. We feel joy, happiness, and satisfaction more often. Greater purpose also leads to less death and heart disease.[143]

Many years of research and data have shown that certain lifestyles benefit from better health, significant medical cost savings, productivity improvements, and increased economic vitality. The data is clear, however: embracing change is challenging and overwhelming. Fortunately we have some real-life examples to learn from.

Blue Zones are areas of the world with a higher than average number of centenarians, where people remain active in their eighties and nineties and do not suffer from the chronic diseases common in most parts of the industrialized world. Blue Zone regions include the Barbagia region of Sardinia, Italy; Ikaria, Greece; Okinawa, Japan; the Nicoya Peninsula in Costa Rica; and Loma Linda, California. The research is fascinating and provides practical applications for our health.[144]

Don't get fooled into thinking that there are serums, short-cuts, genetic advantages, or exclusive location-based secrets. In fact, in places like Okinawa, younger generations are eating a more modern Western-based diet (low nutrition, high calories, fast food) and are seeing the very expensive health problems common in the Western world.[145]

A lifestyle that leads to greater longevity doesn't have to be expensive. The list isn't full of fad diets or expensive supplements. If anything, incorporating strategies into our daily routines will save money. It doesn't cost a single dollar to have close connections with friends and family. Eating less meat saves money at the grocery store. We can change our mind and change our health. Take one area of life that causes stress; maybe it's money, work, or life changes, and think of how to put a positive spin on it. Laugh. As difficult as life can be, laughter is medicine for the soul and the body. Laughter improves our intake of oxygen-rich air, stimulates our hearts, lungs and muscles, and increases the endorphins that are released by our brains.

Richard Eisenberg, investor, editor, and writer, wanted to find out how people in Blue Zones made their money last over such long lives. On a research trip to Costa Rica, he found that the largest cluster of the world's oldest people doesn't worry about money. Most residents are "poor" by American standards and frequently find themselves short of cash.

One person Richard interviewed was Jorge Vindas, founder of the Asociación Península de Nicoya Zona Azul, a nonprofit dedicated to supporting Nicoya Peninsula residents over ninety, especially the poorest ones. When asked what Jorge thought Americans could learn from the oldest residents of the Nicoya Peninsula Blue Zone, he responded: "To copy their lifestyle, which includes eating better, always having physical activity, knowing that family comes first and always having faith in a supreme power. If you put them all together, you will automatically have a better life."[146]

Well-being isn't about accumulating the largest possible pile of money at the expense of everything else in life. The healthcare system will take your money by the millions. At some point, we will all breathe our last breath and no amount of money will change that fact. We can, however, choose to have rich, fulfilling lives, and in the words of my late great friend Chris Hopper, "live with no regrets."

Author J. K. Rowling, author of the Harry Potter series, said, "Family is a life jacket in the stormy sea of life."[147] Life is indeed stormy. Family and friends, our community or the family we choose, play a significant role in our well-being and building whole health wealth.

# MONEY TALK Q&A

## Q: Do I need life insurance?

A: It depends. Ask yourself, "Does anyone rely on my income?" Could they afford the cost of burial, rent or mortgage payments, and other expenses? Could they cover those costs and still maintain their normal life? If anyone needs help to pay expenses after your passing, then consider what type of insurance will be best for your needs.

## Q: How much insurance do I need?

A: Some experts recommend 10 times your annual income. I think the actual amount is personal and nuanced. Consider how many years of income your dependents will need. Multiply that by the annual net income that your survivors will need. Are there any one-time expenses like college or donating to charity? Do you have other saving and investments? Can you afford to pay the premiums?

For an Understanding the Basics of Estate Planning guide and checklist, visit www.MattParadise.com/capablebonus.

# EPILOGUE

# KEEP IT PERSONAL

I'm so excited for you. As this book comes to a close, I pray that your understanding, combined with financial access, behaviors, and knowledge, leads to whole health wealth. We build a wealthy life by investing in the eight key areas of well-being: physical, emotional, intellectual, social, spiritual, environmental, occupational, and financial. I encourage you to share your knowledge, encourage friends and family to practice healthy behaviors, and get involved to foster equitable environments. You'll find it fulfilling, and your increased skills will help loved ones to become financially capable.

In the world of money, there's no shortage of advice and people who will tell you what you "need" to do. In fact, there are many thoughts on what it even means to be rich. If you've read this far, you have your own ideas about living a wealthy life. As we bring this book to a close, I want to impart one last thought: keep personal finance PERSONAL.

**Personal:** We may all be in the same storm in this wild world, but we are not in the same boat. Jeff Bezos, founder of Amazon, has a bigger boat than mine, and that's okay. The strategies he uses aren't necessarily best for me and my family. Similarly, what's best for us may not be the most beneficial for someone else. While there are financial facts and even best practices, we are the masters of our own destiny.

**E**motions: Let's face it, dealing with money is emotional. Life is emotional. And that's not a bad thing. There is joy when receiving a meaningful gift. Love is a powerful emotion. However, many people become anxious or stressed at the thought of balancing a checkbook or saving for the future. The ability to control our feelings helps us to be successful.

**R**esources: There are four economic resource categories: land, labor, capital, and technology/entrepreneurship.[148] Personal resources are the physical or psychological aspects that can help achieve work goals, well-being, and performance.[149] Psychological capital refers to internal capacities of self-efficacy, hope, optimism, and resilience.[150] How we use the resources is personal. And those choices make all the difference.

**S**ave: Building wealth is less about how much we make than about how much we can hold on to. If your goal is to give your wealth away, you still need to build it first. Ronald Read was one person who understood that you don't need a huge income to be wealthy. He was the first in his family to graduate from high school and served in the military during World War II. After the war, he went home to Vermont and worked at a gas station and then as a janitor at a local department store. He lived a simple and frugal life. It's reported that he saved money by cutting his own firewood and wearing old clothes. He was also a disciplined investor. At the time of his death in 2014, Read had built an $8 million fortune and left most of it to the library and hospital in his hometown of Brattleboro, Vermont.[151]

**O**rganize: Staying organized is difficult, but it's necessary. Disorganized finances will lead to missed bill payments and late fees, missed opportunities, stress, and anxiety. How you organize is personal. Find and maintain the system that works for you. If you find the process challenging, it's okay to get help.

**Numbers:** My son has a love/hate relationship with math. He loves counting the money he earns, but hates sitting in math class and finds the subject difficult. He's not alone. Data shows that 82% of students dislike mathematics, and among these students 75% believe that math is a difficult subject.[152] If building wealth is a personal goal, you must conquer your math fears and know your numbers.

**Assets:** Though time and health are our greatest assets, they're often underappreciated until spent. An asset is a valuable resource that we own or control, expecting it will provide a future benefit. Examples include stocks and real estate, and less thought of, but critical physical and mental health assets. Our investments influence the quality of our time. Wealthy people build and gain assets, while those people stuck in patterns of buying stuff and living beyond their means have liabilities and poverty.

**Live and Love Life:** One of my favorite pieces of encouragement came from my wife before we were married. While getting to know each other, I offered to share details about my colorful life. She said, "I don't need to hear about every mistake you've ever made. I love who you are today."

We can't relive the past or correct errors we've made. What we do today builds and defines our futures. You can sow seeds that blossom into your dream life. Becoming financially capable isn't about pursuing the largest pile of cash while forsaking everything else. The end of that road is where loneliness and despair live.

Yes, money can provide the freedom to spend time with loved ones. The love of money, however, is a burden that imprisons. The love of money has caused many marriages to fail and children to be neglected. When money becomes the master, it steals joy and ruins relationships; it increases worries and stress; and it strains our mental and physical health. No one wants to swim in a sea of anxiety. Do you know what research says is the #1 thing we can do to become happier? "Invest in relationships with other people."[153]

Take a deep breath. Love life and live.

# URGENT REQUEST

Thank you so much for reading this book! I'd love to hear what you have to say. Your input is valuable and can help other people become financially capable.

Will you please take a moment to leave an honest review for this book on Amazon or wherever you purchased it? Reviews are the best way to help as many as possible learn about this helpful information.

I appreciate you!

With sincere gratitude,

Matt Paradise

# Claim your free
# financially capable book bonuses.

Go to www.MattParadise.com/capablebonus
for these valuable resources:

Your Money Type Test

*Family Budget/Economic Security Calculator*

Predatory Financial Products and Services Guide

*The Consumer Financial Emergency Survival Kit*

Age Differences in Consumer Financial Capability Study

*First Money Memory Worksheet*

Budget Worksheet

*The Investment Risk Tolerance Quiz*

How to Access Consumer Reporting Companies Booklet

*Credit Score Booklet*

Identity Theft Guide

*Guide to Saving and Investing*

Access to Online Courses

*and more!*

# ACKNOWLEDGMENTS

Relationships influence and forge our personal and professional lives. Isaac Newton said, "If I have seen further, it is by standing upon the shoulders of giants." I'm incredibly grateful for the many people who have let me stand on their shoulders and helped to forge the person I am today. First and foremost, thank you to God. I'm sustained by grace.

Thank you to the many Jump$tart Coalition colleagues: Laura Levine, Dan Hebert, Declan Sheehy, Larry Glazer, Margaret Brooks, and Bill Cheeks, to name a few. The Midas/MFEC/MassSaves crew: Margaret Miley, Scott Guild, Dave Floreen, Kerri McLaughlin, Jacqueline Cooper, Kimberly Zimmerman Rand. To think, we went from nothing to creating legislation for all K–12 students!

Thank you to American Consumer Credit Counseling and my many great colleagues over the years. Clete Thomas and Sue Katz for helping to spread financial education far and wide. Amy, you've been like a more mature sister. Donna, I will never forget your enduring kindness. Katie and Tracey, your support means the world to me. Allen, you believed in me when others didn't. And to Steve Trumble, who gave a nineteen-year-old kid a chance, I'm forever grateful for your mentorship. May your soul find rest.

Paul Horwitz and Kipp Child, your mentorship and encouragement have been invaluable. Trinh Nguyen, Constance Martin, Mimi Turchinetz, Allen Gentle, and the entire

Office of Financial Empowerment team, thanks for working to ensure that the "arc of the moral universe bends toward justice."

Thank you to George Araneo, Debbie Paolillo, Brett Peruzzi, Korrina Jamison, Natalia Monsalve, Shannen Amicangioli, Shelby Janke, Laura Starling, Deborah Lang, Ben Bushart, Kristen Small, Sandra Wendel, Alice Douthwaite, Chris Shannon, and Honorée Corder for your invaluable advice, mentorship, and encouragement during the creation of this book.

Words can't do justice for the gratitude I have for the medical teams who helped me conquer cholangiocarcinoma. Dr. Casey and Dr. Krishnan, your endoscopes are legendary. Dr. Nipp, your empathy and expertise brought comfort during the most challenging times. If you can help it, radiation is best avoided. If you need it, Dr. Wo is amazing. Dr. Andersson, you brought clarity to the chaos; thank you for your advocacy. Dr. Sise, losing kidney function is kind of a bummer, but your responsiveness brought me back. Dr. Dua, God willing, the readers won't need a vascular surgeon, but you're amazing; thanks for keeping the blood flowing. Dr. Kotton, infectious disease sounds scary, but you helped preserve my life. Dr. Kimura, your steady hand gave me more than a liver; it gave a boy his father, and a woman her husband.

There are hundreds who encouraged me, sat by my side, and nursed me to health. Brenda, Stephanie, Judy, Ashley, Colleen, and so many more. Saying thanks seems to fall short. You have my sincerest enduring gratitude.

I'm a believer that "no debt should remain outstanding, except the continuing debt to love one another." The following people have supported me through thick and thin, cancer and health: Steve and Pam Major, Lonnie and Earlina Jamison,

Mike and Scarlette Van Auken, Greg and Yvonne Chalmers, Tim and Celeste Montgomery, Julie Beckham, Shin and Kin Mak, Paul and Rhonda Paradise (a.k.a. Mom and Dad), Gosia Tomaszewska, Nika Elugardo, and many friends and family. Thank you for your loving support. Most of all, words can't fully express the gratitude I have for my wife. Elsa, without you this book wouldn't be possible.

And for every single person I've had the privilege of coaching and teaching, you've taught me more than you'll ever know. Thank you.

# REFERENCES

1   Capital One. 2021. "Financial Well Being Study Findings." July 30.
    https://www.capitalone.com/about/newsroom/financial-well-being-
    study-findings/.

2   Environmental Protection Agency, EPA. 2022. "Sustainable Management
    of Food." July 7. https://www.epa.gov/sustainable-management-food/
    united-states-2030-food-loss-and-waste-reduction-goal.

3   Director of National Intelligence. 2023. "This Security Executive Agent
    (SecEA) Directive 4." *Office of the Director of National Intelligence.*
    January 27. https://www.dni.gov/files/NCSC/documents/Regulations/
    SEAD-4-Adjudicative-Guidelines-U.pdf.

4   Statista. 2023. *Economy.* January. https://www.statista.com/
    statistics/299460/distribution-of-wealth-in-the-united-
    states/#statisticContainer.

5   Obama, Michelle. 2018. *Becoming.* New York: Crown Publishing
    Group.

6   Pfeffer, Susan Beth. 2011. *This World We live In.* New York: Clarion
    Books.

7   Smith, Monica M. 2022. *LEMELSON CENTER for the Study of
    Invention and Innovation.* February 21. Accessed January 2023. https://
    invention.si.edu/diverse-voices-inventor-garrett-morgan.

8   Vella, Christina. 2022. *George Washington Carver: A Life.* Louisiana:
    Louisiana State University Press.

9   Thaler, Richard H. 2021. *Nudge: Improving Decisions About Health,
    Wealth, and Happiness (The Final Edition).* London: Penguin Books.

10  Cronkite, Walter, interview by American Library Association "Libraries
    Change Lives" Campaign. 1995. *Libraries Change Lives Campaign.*

11  Brookline Public Library. n.d. *Sensitive Subjects by Location.* Accessed
    2023. https://www.dracutlibrary.org/sensitive-subjects-by-location/.

12  Wille, Jacklyn. 2020. *Bloomberg Law.* August 31. Accessed 2022. https://
    news.bloomberglaw.com/employee-benefits/401k-fee-suits-flood-courts-
    on-pace-for-fivefold-jump-in-2020.

13  US Dept of Labor. 1974. *Employee Retirement Income Security Act
    (ERISA).* Accessed 2022. https://www.dol.gov/general/topic/retirement/
    erisa.

14  Todd, Jonathan and Dayana Yochim. 2016. *NerdWallet.* April 27.
    Accessed 2022. https://www.nerdwallet.com/blog/investing/millennial-
    retirement-fees-one-percent-half-million-savings-impact/.

[15] Personal Capital. n.d. "Advisor fee Report." *Personal Capital.* Accessed 2022. https://www.personalcapital.com/assets/public/src/Personal-Capital-Advisor-Fee-Report.pdf.

[16] Hanson, Melanie. 2022. *Education Data Initiative.* October 26. https://educationdata.org/student-loan-debt-statistics.

[17] Serani, Deborah. 2011. *Psychology Today.* June 7. Accessed 2022. https://www.psychologytoday.com/us/blog/two-takes-depression/201106/if-it-bleeds-it-leads-understanding-fear-based-media.

[18] Yaffe-Belany, David, Erin Griffith and Ephrat Livni. 2022. *New York Times.* May 12. Accessed 2022. https://www.nytimes.com/2022/05/12/technology/cryptocurrencies-crash-bitcoin.html.

[19] La Monica, Paul R. 2022. *CNN Business.* May 12. Accessed 2022. https://www.cnn.com/2022/05/12/investing/stocks-bear-market/index.html.

[20] Glassner, Barry. 2010. *The Culture of Fear: Why Americans Are Afraid of the Wrong Things: Crime, Drugs, Minorities, Teen Moms, Killer Kids, Mutant Microbes, Plane Crashes, Road Rage, & So Much More.* New York: Basic Books.
History.com Editors. 2023. *Great Depression History.* A&E Television Networks. January 12. https://www.history.com/topics/great-depression/great-depression-history.
Galbraith, John Kenneth. 2009. *The Great Crash 1929.* New York: Harper Business.

[21] Franklin, Benjamin. 1980. *Poor Richard's Almanack.* Mount Vernon: Peter Pauper Press.

[22] Wilde, Oscar. 2003. *The Picture of Dorian Gray.* London: Penguin Classics.

[23] Federal Reserve Bank of Boston. n.d. *Working Cities Challenge.* Accessed 2022. https://www.bostonfed.org/community-development/supporting-growth-in-smaller-industrial-cities/working-cities-challenge.aspx.

[24] Federal Deposit Insurance Corporation. n.d. "When a Bank Fails - Facts for Depositors, Creditors, and Borrowers." Accessed 2022. https://www.fdic.gov/consumers/banking/facts/.

[25] United States Government. n.d. *Financial Crimes Enforcement Network.* https://www.fincen.gov/financial-institution-definition.

[26] Cboe Exchange, Inc. 2023. "U.S. Equities Market Volume Summary." https://www.cboe.com/us/equities/market_share/.

[27] Kenton, Will. 2021. "Financial Instruments Explained: Types and Asset Classes." *Investopedia.* August 29. Accessed 2022. https://www.investopedia.com/terms/f/financialinstrument.asp.
Corporation, Federal Deposit Insurance. 2022. *Money Smart.* October 12. https://www.fdic.gov/resources/consumers/money-smart/index.html.

Financial Industry Regulatory Authority (FINRA). n.d. *For Investors-Investment Products*. Accessed 2023. https://www.finra.org/investors/investing/investment-products.

28    Shmoop. 2023. *Money: The Economic Definition*. https://www.shmoop.com/money-banking/economic-definition.html#:~:text=Money%20is%20a%20medium%20of,for%20identifying%20and%20communicating%20value.

29    1 Tim 6:10 KJV.
Nance-Nash, Sheryl. n.d. "Is The Bible The Ultimate Financial Guide?" *Forbes Woman*. Accessed 2022. https://www.forbes.com/sites/sherylnancenash/2012/05/24/is-the-bible-the-ultimate-financial-guide/?sh=4213e4766493 .

30    McConnell, Campbell, Stanley Brue, Sean Flynn. 2014. *Macroeconomics: Principles, Problems, & Policies 20th Edition*. New York: McGraw Hill.
Krugman, Paul, Robin Wells. 2021. *Macroeconomics Sixth Edition*. New York: Worth Publishers.

31    Khan Academy. 2023. *Microeconomics*. https://www.khanacademy.org/economics-finance-domain/microeconomics.
Mankiw, N. Gregory. 2014. *Principles of Microeconomics, 7th Edition*. Boston: Cengage Learning.

32    The World Bank. n.d. *Understanding Poverty Macroeconomics*. Accessed 2022. https://www.worldbank.org/en/topic/macroeconomics.

33    Delaney, Kevin J., Allison Schrager. 2019. "Dismal Science." *Quartz*. 17 September. Accessed 2021. https://qz.com/1709972/bill-gates-economists-dont-actually-understand-macroeconomics.

34    Persky, Joseph. 1995. "Retrospectives: The Ethology of Homo economicus." *The Journal of Economic Perspectives, Vol. 9, No. 2* 221–231.
Edward J. O'Boyle. 2010. *Mayo Research Institute*. March 10. https://mayoresearch.org/files/ORIGINS%20HOMO%20ECONOMICUS%20mar102010.pdf.

35    Ariely, Dan. 2010. *Predictably Irrational: The Hidden Forces That Shape Our Decisions*. New York: Harper Perennial.

36    Commission, Australian Human Rights. n.d. *What is Racism?* Accessed 2023. https://humanrights.gov.au/our-work/race-discrimination/what-racism.

37    Krueger, Alan B., Adam Smith. 2009 [1776]. *The Wealth of Nations*. Seattle: Thrifty Books.

38    Beja, Bongiwe. 2020. "Changemakers." *Real Leaders Magazine*. February 4. Accessed 2021. https://real-leaders.com/the-african-concept-of-ubuntu-should-be-at-the-heart-of-human-rights/.

39    Yam, Kimmy. 2022. "NBC News." *Asian America*. February 14. Accessed March 2022. https://www.nbcnews.com/news/asian-america/

anti-asian-hate-crimes-increased-339-percent-nationwide-last-year-repo-rcna14282.

[40] Fairlie, Robert W. 2020. "The Impact of Covid-19 on Small Business Owners: Evidence of Early-Stage Losses from." *NBER Working Paper No. 27309 JEL No. J15,J16,L26.* June. https://www.nber.org/system/files/working_papers/w27309/w27309.pdf.

[41] Braveman, Paula A., Elaine Arkin, Dwayne Proctor, Tina Kauh, and Nicole Holm. 2022. "Systemic And Structural Racism: Definitions, Examples, Health Damages, And Approaches To Dismantling." *Health Affairs VOL. 41, NO. 2: Racism & Health.* February. https://www.healthaffairs.org/doi/10.1377/hlthaff.2021.01394.

[42] Banaji, Mahzarin R., Susan T. Fiske, and Douglas S. Massey. 2021. "Systemic racism: individuals and interactions, institutions and society." *Cognitive research: principles and implications* vol. 6,1 82. 20 Dec. 2021.

[43] Aliprantis, Dionissi, Daniel R. Carroll. 2019. "What Is Behind the Persistence of the Racial Wealth Gap?" *Federal Reserve Bank of Cleveland.* February. https://www.clevelandfed.org/publications/economic-commentary/2019/ec-201903-what-is-behind-the-persistence-of-the-racial-wealth-gap.
Emanuel Nieves. 2017. "New Report Finds Racial Wealth Inequality A Growing National Emergency." *Prosperity Now.* September 14. https://prosperitynow.org/blog/new-report-finds-racial-wealth-inequality-growing-national-emergency.
Collins, Chuck, Dedrick Asante-Muhammad, Josh Hoxie, Sabrina Terry. 2019. "How Enriching the 1% Widens the Racial Wealth Divide." *Institute for Policy Studies.* https://inequality.org/wp-content/uploads/2019/01/IPS_RWD-Report_FINAL-1.15.19.pdf.

[44] Peterson, Dana M., Catherine L Mann. 2020. "Closing the Racial Inequality Gaps: The Economic Cost of Black Inequality in the U.S." *Citi Global Perspectives & Solutions.* September. https://www.citivelocity.com/citigps/closing-the-racial-inequality-gaps/.

[45] Losavio, Joseph. 2020. "What Racism Costs Us All." *International Monetary Fund.* September. https://www.imf.org/en/Publications/fandd/issues/2020/09/the-economic-cost-of-racism-losavio.

[46] Shrider, Emily A., Melissa Kollar, Frances Chen, and Jessica Semega. 2021. "Income and Poverty in the United States Report Number P60-273." *United States Census Bureau.* September 14. https://www.census.gov/library/publications/2021/demo/p60-273.html.

[47] Bertrand, Marianne, Sendhil Mullainathan. n.d. "Are Emily and Greg More Employable than Lakisha and Jamal? A Field Experiment on Labor Market Discrimination Working Paper 9873 DOI 10.3386/w9873." *National Bureau of Economic Research.* Accessed January 2023. https://www.nber.org/papers/w9873.

48   Judicial Branch of the U.S. Government. n.d. "The Plessy Decision."
     *United States Courts.* Accessed 2023. https://www.uscourts.gov/
     educational-resources/educational-activities/history-brown-v-board-
     education-re-enactment.

49   García, Emma. 2020. "Schools are still segregated, and black children
     are paying a price." *Economic Policy Institute.* February 12. https://www.
     epi.org/publication/schools-are-still-segregated-and-black-children-are-
     paying-a-price/.

50   Nathan, Linda F. n.d. "Systemic Inequity." *New England Board of Higher
     Education.* Accessed February 2023. https://nebhe.org/journal/systemic-
     inequity/.

51   Navient Multi-State Settlement. 2022. "39 State Attorneys
     General Announce $1.85 Billion Settlement with Student Loan
     Servicer Navient." *Navient AG Multi-State Settlement* . July 29. https://
     navientagsettlement.com/Home/portalid/0.

52   Reeves, Richard V., Ariel Gelrud Shiro. 2021. "How We Rise." *The
     Brookings Institution.* January 12. https://www.brookings.edu/blog/how-
     we-rise/2021/01/12/the-for-profit-college-system-is-broken-and-the-
     biden-administration-needs-to-fix-it/.

53   US Department of Education. 2022. "Education Department Approves
     $415 Million in Borrower Defense Claims Including for Former DeVry
     University Students." *US Department of Education.* February 16. https://
     www.ed.gov/news/press-releases/education-department-approves-415-
     million-borrower-defense-claims-including-former-devry-university-
     students.

54   Supreme Court of the United States. n.d. "Milestone Documents Brown
     v. Board of Education (1954)." *National Archives.* Accessed January 30,
     2023. https://www.archives.gov/milestone-documents/brown-v-board-
     of-education.

55   US Census Bureau. 2020. "Homeownership rates show that Black
     Americans are currently the least likely group to own homes." *USA
     Facts.* October 16. Accessed 2023. https://usafacts.org/articles/
     homeownership-rates-by-race/.

56   Rothstein, Richard. 2018. *The Color of Law: A Forgotten History of How
     Our Government Segregated America.* New York: Norton & Company,
     Inc.

57   Caves, Roger W. (Editor). 2013. *Encyclopedia of the City.* Oxfordshire:
     Routledge.

58   Austin Turner, Margery, Rob Santos, Diane K. Levy, Doug Wissoker,
     Claudia Aranda, Rob Pitingolo. 2013. "U.S. Department of Housing
     and Urban Development." *Office of Policy Development and Research.*
     June. Accessed January 2023. https://www.huduser.gov/portal/
     Publications/pdf/HUD-514_HDS2012.pdf.

59  US Department of Justice Office of Public Affairs. 2023. "Press Release Number 23-33." *U.S. Department of Justice.* January 12. https://www. justice.gov/opa/pr/justice-department-secures-over-31-million-city- national-bank-address-lending-discrimination.

60  Morris, Gouverneur. 1787. *The Constitution of the United States, Preamble.* September 17. Accessed February 22, 2023. https://www. archives.gov/founding-docs/constitution-transcript.

61  Roosevelt, Eleanor. 1958. "Remarks at the United Nations." *United Nations.* March 27. Accessed January 2023. https://www.un.org/ en/%E2%80%9Cclose-home%E2%80%9D-universal-declaration- human-rights-0.

62  Kollárik, Martin, Marcel van den Hout, Carlotta V. Heinzel, Patrizia D. Hofer, Roselind Lieb, and Karina Wahl. 2020. "Effects of rumination on unwanted intrusive thoughts: A replication and extension." *Journal of Experimental Psychopathology* doi:10.1177/2043808720912583.

63  Northwestern University Health Promotion and Wellness. n.d. *Eight Dimensions of Wellness Overview.* Accessed February 2023. https://www. northwestern.edu/wellness/8-dimensions/.

64  Solomon, Deborah. An interview of Desmond Tutu. 2010. *The Priest. New York Times Magazine.* March 4. http://www.nytimes. com/2010/03/07/magazine/07fob-q4-t.html.

65  Stanford GSB Staff. 2005. "Insights by Stanford Business Baba Shiv: Emotions Can Negatively Impact Investment Decisions." September 1. Accessed January 2023. https://www.gsb.stanford.edu/insights/baba- shiv-emotions-can-negatively-impact-investment-decisions. Palmer, Kimberly. 2022. "Why Managing Your Money Starts With Your Emotions." June 9. Accessed January 2023. https://www.nerdwallet. com/article/finance/why-managing-your-money-starts-with-your- emotions.

66  Wiesel, Elie. 1986. "Hope, Despair and Memory." Nobel lecture. Oslo, December 11.

67  Schwartz, Shalom H. 2012. "An Overview of the Schwartz Theory of Basic Values." *The Hebrew University of Jerusalem. Online Readings in Psychology and Culture,* 2(1). https://doi.org/10.9707/2307-0919.1116.

68  Cleveland Clinic. 2021. *Health Essentials: Why Retail "Therapy" Makes You Feel Happier.* January 21. Accessed January 31, 2023. https://health. clevelandclinic.org/retail-therapy-shopping-compulsion/.

69  *Psychology Today* Staff. n.d. *What Is Addiction?* Accessed January 2023. https://www.psychologytoday.com/us/basics/addiction.

70  Machado, Sara, Andrew Sumarsono, Muthiah Vaduganathan. 2021. "Midlife Wealth Mobility and Long-term Cardiovascular Health." *JAMA Cardiology* 6(10):1152–1160. doi:10.1001/jamacardio.2021.2056.

71 Mullainathan, Sendhil, Eldar Shafir. 2013. *Scarcity: Why Having Too Little Means So Much.* New York: Times Books.

72 National Institute on Alcohol Abuse and Alcoholism. 2022. *Alcohol's Effects on Health.* March. Accessed January 2023. https://www.niaaa.nih. gov/publications/brochures-and-fact-sheets/alcohol-facts-and-statistics.

73 Sussman, Steve, Nadra Lisha, Mark Griffiths. 2011. "Prevalence of the addictions: a problem of the majority or the minority?" *Evaluation & the Health Professions* 34(1):3-56. doi: 10.1177/0163278710380124. Epub 2010 Sep 27. PMID: 20876085; PMCID: PMC3134413.

74 Wilson, Edward Osborne. 1999. *Consilience: The Unity of Knowledge.* New York: Vintage.

75 The Decision Lab. n.d. "Bias: Why are we likely to continue with an investment even if it would be rational to give it up?" Accessed February 1, 2023. https://thedecisionlab.com/biases/the-sunk-cost-fallacy.

76 Farber, Madeline. 2016. "Finance: Economy: Nearly Two-Thirds of Americans Can't Pass a Basic Test of Financial Literacy." *Forbes.* July 12. Accessed February 2023. https://fortune.com/2016/07/12/financial-literacy/.

77 National Foundation for Credit Counseling® (NFCC®). n.d. "Client impact and research." *2019 Consumer Financial Literacy Survey.* Accessed February 2023. https://digital.nfcc.org/resources/client-impact-and-research/2019-consumer-financial-literacy-survey/.

78 NextGen Personal Finance. n.d. "NGPF's 2022 State of Financial Education Report." *NGPF Annual Report.* Accessed February 2023. https://d3f7q2msm2165u.cloudfront.net/aaa-content/user/files/Files/NGPFAnnualReport_2022.pdf.

79 Klapper, Leora, Annamaria Lusardi, Peter van Oudheusden. n.d. "Financial Literacy Around the World: Insights From the Standard and Poor's Ratings Services Global Financial Literacy Survey." *The George Washington School of Business: Global Financial Literacy Excellence Center.* Accessed February 2023. https://gflec.org/wp-content/uploads/2015/11/3313-Finlit_Report_FINAL-5.11.16.pdf.

80 Urban, Carly, Olivia Valdes. 2022. "FINRA Investor Education Insights: Financial Capability." *FINRA Investor Education Foundation.* August. https://www.finrafoundation.org/sites/finrafoundation/files/Insights-Why-is-Measured-Financial-Literacy-Declining.pdf.

81 Consumer Financial Protection Bureau (CFPB). n.d. "Navigating the Market: A comparison of spending on financial education and financial marketing." Accessed February 2023. https://files.consumerfinance. gov/f/201311_cfpb_navigating-the-market-final.pdf.

82 Ibid.

83 Open Secrets. n.d. "Finance/Insurance/Real Estate: Lobbying, 2022." *Lobbying profile for Finance/Insurance/Real Estate.* Accessed February 1, 2023. https://www.opensecrets.org/industries/lobbying.php?ind=F.

84   Grassley, Senator. Chuck, [R-IA]. 2005. "S.256 Bankruptcy Abuse
     Prevention and Consumer Protection Act of 2005." *United States
     Congress.* April 20. https://www.congress.gov/bill/109th-congress/senate-
     bill/256.

85   Greenya, John. 2017. "Economics: Bankruptcy Reform's Poor Legacy."
     *Pacific Standard Magazine.* June 14. Accessed February 1, 2023. https://
     psmag.com/economics/bankruptcy-reforms-poor-legacy-4204.

86   Ibid.

87   Ibid.

88   Ibid.

89   Ferraro, Thomas. 2009. "AIG chief says 'I need all the help I can get.'"
     *Reuters Business News.* March 18. Accessed February 2023. https://www.
     reuters.com/article/uk-financial-aig-scene-sb/aig-chief-says-i-need-all-
     the-help-i-can-get-idUKTRE52I02S20090319.

90   Frank, Representative Barney [D-MA-4] . 2009-2010. "United States
     Congress." *H.R.4173 - Dodd-Frank Wall Street Reform and Consumer
     Protection Act.* Accessed February 2023. https://www.congress.gov/
     bill/111th-congress/house-bill/4173/text.

91   Lusardi, Annamaria. George Washington University School of
     Business. 2019. "It's time for colleges to require mandated financial
     literacy courses." June. Accessed February 2023. https://www.cnbc.
     com/2019/06/25/its-time-for-colleges-to-require-mandated-financial-
     literacy-courses.html.

92   Ezarik, Melissa. 2022. "Student Voice: Where the Weaknesses Are in
     Student Financial Wellness." *Inside Higher ED.* February 25. Accessed
     February 1, 2023. https://www.insidehighered.com/news/2022/02/25/
     survey-college-students-need-help-financial-literacy.

93   Buscaglia, Leo. 1972. *Love: A Warm and Wonderful Book About the
     Largest Experience in Life.* Robbinsdale: Fawcett Crest.

94   Delgado, Michelle. n.d. "The Pandemic Has Plunged Americans
     Into Severe Credit Card Debt: 2021 Data." *1031 Exchange.* Accessed
     February 2023. https://inside1031.com/credit-card-debt-2021/.

95   United States Internal Revenue Service (IRS). n.d. "Free Tax Return
     Preparation for Qualifying Taxpayers." Accessed February 2023. https://
     www.irs.gov/individuals/free-tax-return-preparation-for-qualifying-
     taxpayers.

96   United Way of Massachusetts Bay and Merrimack Valley, the City of
     Boston, and LISC Boston. n.d. *Boston Builds Credit.* Accessed February
     2023. https://www.bostonbuildscredit.org/.

97   Kaplan, Greg, Giovanni L. Violante, Justin Weidner. 2014. "Working
     Paper 20073 DOI 10.3386/w20073 The Wealthy Hand-to-Mouth."
     *Brookings Papers on Economic Activity.* April. https://www.nber.org/
     papers/w20073.

98   Ibid.

[99] Stanley, Thomas J., William D. Danko. 2010. *The Millionaire Next Door: The Surprising Secrets of America's Wealthy.* Boulder: Taylor Trade Publishing.

[100] Brown, Leanne. 2015. *Good and Cheap: Eat Well on $4/Day.* New York: Workman Publishing Company.

[101] Intuit, Inc. 2023. *Mint Managing money, made simple.* Accessed February 2023. https://mint.intuit.com/.

[102] Consumer Financial Protection Bureau (CFPB). n.d. *Resources for small business owners.* Accessed Janruary 2023. https://www.consumerfinance.gov/about-us/small-business-lending/additional-resources/.
U.S. Department of Treasury. n.d. *Small Business Resources.* Accessed Janruary 2023. https://home.treasury.gov/policy-issues/small-business-programs/small-and-disadvantaged-business-utilization/small-business-resources.
Jessica Elliott. US Chamber of Commerce. n.d. "10 Free Resources for Small Businesses to Leverage Year-Round." Accessed Janruary 2023. https://www.uschamber.com/co/start/strategy/free-resources-for-small-businesses.
Colwell, Ken. 2019. *Starting a Business QuickStart Guide: The Simplified Beginner's Guide to Launching a Successful Small Business, Turning Your Vision into Reality, and ... Dream.* Albany: ClydeBank Media LLC; Illustrated edition.

[103] Goldman, Robert and Papson, Stephen. 1998. *Nike Culture: The Sign of the Swoosh.* SAGE Publications Ltd.

[104] Hughes, Langston. May 1922. *Dreams.* New York: The Fellowship Press, Inc. Printed in *The World Tomorrow* magazine.

[105] Lachard, James J. (Jim Brown.) I dreamed I had an interview with God. n.d. *Center for Global Leadership.* Accessed February 2, 2023. https://centerforgloballeadership.wordpress.com/2012/06/30/an-interview-with-god-i-stand-corrected/.

[106] Herrick, Dr. Charles. 2020. "Nuvance Health: Why We Make (and Break) New Year's Resolutions, and 4 Tips to Help You Achieve Your Goals." January 16. Accessed February 2023. https://www.newswise.com/articles/why-we-make-and-break-new-year-s-resolutions-and-4-tips-to-help-you-achieve-your-goals.

[107] Vega, Nicolas. 2022. "Save and Invest: Warren Buffett says 'monkeys' could do as good a job investing as Wall Street financial advisors." *CNBC.* May 2. Accessed February 2, 2023. https://www.cnbc.com/2022/05/02/warren-buffett-says-investing-is-a-simple-game.html.

[108] Backman, Maurie. 2016. "A Cat Outperformed Pro Stock-Pickers. Here's What That Means for Investors." *Motley Fool.* August 1. Accessed 2 2022, February. https://www.fool.com/investing/2016/08/01/a-cat-outperformed-pro-stock-pickers-heres-what-th.aspx.

[109]  Kennedy, John Fitzgerald. n.d. "House Appropriations Subcommittee on Defense Holds Hearing on DOD Continuing Resolutions." *United States Navy.* Accessed February 2, 2023. https://www.navy.mil/Press-Office/Testimony/display-testimony/Article/2905235/house-appropriations-subcommittee-on-defense-holds-hearing-on-dod-continuing-re/.

[110]  Fidelity Investments. Q2 2022. "Participant Well-being Survey." *Building Financial Futures: Trends and insights of those saving for retirement across America.* Accessed February 2023. https://institutional.fidelity.com/app/proxy/content?literatureURL=/9892751.PDF.

[111]  Barber, Brad M., Yi-Tsung Lee, Yu-Jane Liu, Terrance Odean. March 2014. "The cross-section of speculator skill: Evidence from day trading." *Journal of Financial Markets Volume 18* 1-24.

Chague, Fernando. Rodrigo De-Losso, Bruno Giovannetti. June 15 2020. "Day Trading for a Living?" *Social Science Research Network (SSRN).* Available at SSRN: https://ssrn.com/abstract=3423101 or http://dx.doi.org/10.2139/ssrn.3423101.

Barber, Brad M., Xing Huang, Terrance Odean, Christopher Schwarz. 2021. "Attention Induced Trading and Returns: Evidence from Robinhood Users." *Journal of Finance.* Available at SSRN: https://ssrn.com/abstract=3715077 .

[112]  Holupka, Scott, Sandra J. Newman. 2012. "The Effects of Homeownership on Children's Outcomes: Real Effects or Self-Selection?" *Real Estate Economics* 40(3), 566-602. https://doi.org/10.1111/j.1540-6229.2012.00330.x.

[113]  Stokel-Walker, Chris. 2021. "How a Squid Game Crypto Scam Got Away With Millions." *Wired.* November 2. Accessed February 2, 2023. https://www.wired.com/story/squid-game-coin-crypto-scam/.

[114]  Lewis, Antony. 2018. *The Basics of Bitcoins and Blockchains: An Introduction to Cryptocurrencies and the Technology that Powers Them (Cryptography, Derivatives Investments, Futures Trading, Digital Assets, NFT).* Miami: Mango.

[115]  Ammous, Saifedean. 2018. *The Bitcoin Standard: The Decentralized Alternative to Central Banking.* Hoboken: Wiley.

[116]  Walker, Ian. 2021. "Kotaku: Someone Right-Clicked Every NFT In The Heist Of The Century: A unique performance art project shows just how useless NFTs can be." November 18. Accessed February 2, 2023. https://kotaku.com/someone-right-clicked-every-nft-in-the-heist-of-the-cen-1848084379.

[117]  Flyfish Club. n.d. *How it Works: Introduction: Why NFT?* Accessed February 2, 2023. https://www.flyfishclub.com/how-it-works.

[118]  The White House: Presidential Action. 2022. *Executive Order on Ensuring Responsible Development of Digital Assets.* March 9. Accessed February 2, 2023. https://www.whitehouse.gov/briefing-room/

presidential-actions/2022/03/09/executive-order-on-ensuring-
responsible-development-of-digital-assets/.

[119] Harvard Medical School. 2020. *The high cost of a poor diet.* May 1.
Accessed February 9, 2023. https://www.health.harvard.edu/heart-
health/the-high-cost-of-a-poor-diet.

[120] Lynch, Peter, John Rothchild. 1994. *Beating the Street.* Manhattan:
Simon & Schuster.

[121] Banker, S., D. Dunfield, A. Huang et al. 2021. "Neural mechanisms
of credit card spending." *Scientific Reports* 11, Article number: 4070.
https://doi.org/10.1038/s41598-021-83488-3.

[122] HR Research Institute and Professional Background Screening
Association. 2021. "Background Screening: Trends in the U.S. and
Abroad." Accessed February 3, 2023. https://pubs.thepbsa.org/pub.
cfm?id=FB36B937-C9D5-A941-7720-4047386F38B0.

[123] Ejaz, Syed. 2021. "A Broken System: How The Credit Reporting System
Fails Consumers And What To Do About It." *Consumer Reports Credit
Checkup Study.* https://advocacy.consumerreports.org/wp-content
/uploads/2021/06/A-Broken-System-How-the-Credit-Reporting-
System-Fails-Consumers-and-What-to-Do-About-It.pdf. https://
advocacy.consumerreports.org/wp-content/uploads/2021/06/A-Broken-
System-How-the-Credit-Reporting-System-Fails-Consumers-and-What-
to-Do-About-It.pdf.

[124] Mineo, Liz. June 29, 2022. "'Shadow pandemic' of domestic violence."
*The Harvard Gazette: National and World Affairs.* https://news.harvard.
edu/gazette/story/2022/06/shadow-pandemic-of-domestic-violence/.

[125] Noël, Alyson. 2009. *Evermore: The Immortals (The Immortals, 1).* New
York: St. Martin's Griffin.

[126] Dworsky, Amy, Laura Napolitano, Mark Courtney, 2013.
"Homelessness During the Transition From Foster Care to Adulthood."
*American Journal of Public Health* vol. 103 Suppl 2, Suppl 2: S318-23.
doi:10.2105/AJPH.2013.301455.

[127] Quinn, Tom. 2022. *The Perfect Credit Score: Understanding the 850
FICO Score.* April 11. Accessed February 3, 2023. https://www.fico.com/
blogs/perfect-credit-score-understanding-850-fico-score.

[128] Akin, Jim. 2020. "What Are the Different Credit Scoring Ranges?"
*Experian.* June 23. Accessed February 10, 2023. https://www.experian.
com/blogs/ask-experian/infographic-what-are-the-different-scoring-
ranges/.

[129] Abagnale, Frank W., Stan Redding. 2000. *Catch Me If You Can: The
True Story of a Real Fake.* New York: Crown.

[130] Bekker, Eugene. 2021. "What are Your Odds of Getting Your Identity
Stolen?" *IdentityForce, a TransUnion Brand.* April 15. Accessed February

6, 2023. https://www.identityforce.com/blog/identity-theft-odds-identity-theft-statistics.

[131] Buzzard, John. 2022. "2022 Identity Fraud Study: The Virtual Battleground." *Javelin Strategy & Research*. March 29. Accessed February 6, 2023. https://javelinstrategy.com/2022-Identity-fraud-scams-report#:~:text=Javelin's%202022%20Identity%20Fraud%20Study,means%20of%20controlling%20identity%20fraud.

[132] U.S. Department of Health & Human Services. n.d. "Seat Belts." *Centers For Disease Control and Prevention*. Accessed February 6, 2023. https://www.cdc.gov/transportationsafety/seatbelts/index.html.

[133] Schwartz, Elaine. 2020. "Financial Markets: Where Lego is More Than a Toy." *econlife*. September 20. Accessed February 10, 2023. https://econlife.com/2020/09/roi-and-investing-in-legos/.

[134] Suggitt, Connie. 2022. "The $5 million Pokémon card: Inside Logan Paul's record-breaking trade." *Guinness World Records*. July 22. Accessed February 10, 2023. https://www.guinnessworldrecords.com/news/2022/7/the-5-million-pokemon-card-inside-logan-pauls-record-breaking-trade-708581#:~:text=On%202%20April%202022%2C%20at,%C2%A33%2C862%2C424%20%2F%20%E2%82%AC4%2C477%2C146).

[135] Cobb, Daniel. 2022. "2022 Wills and Estate Planning Study." *Caring.com*. Accessed February 6, 2023. https://www.caring.com/caregivers/estate-planning/wills-survey/.

[136] Girvan, Gregg, Avik Roy. 2021. "A startling statistic has profound implications for the way we've managed the coronavirus pandemic." *The Foundation for Research on Equal Opportunity*. January 30. Accessed February 6, 2023. https://freopp.org/the-covid-19-nursing-home-crisis-by-the-numbers-3a47433c3f70.

[137] Office of Disease Prevention and Health Promotion. n.d. "Social Determinants of Health: Healthy People 2030." *US Dept. Health and Human Services*. Accessed 2023. https://health.gov/healthypeople/priority-areas/social-determinants-health.

[138] Ramakrishnan, Rema, Jian-Rong He, Anne-Louise Ponsonby, Mark Woodward, Kazem Rahimi, Steven N. Blair, Terence Dwyer. 2021. "Objectively measured physical activity and all cause mortality: A systematic review and meta-analysis." *Preventive Medicine* Volume 143, February, 106356.

[139] Aune, Dagfinn, Edward Giovannucci, Paolo Boffetta, Lars T Fadnes, NaNa Keum, Teresa Norat, Darren C Greenwood, Elio Riboli, Lars J Vatten, Serena Tonstad. 2017. "Fruit and vegetable intake and the risk of cardiovascular disease, total cancer and all-cause mortality—a systematic review and dose-response meta-analysis of prospective studies." *International Journal of Epidemiology* Volume 46, Issue 3, June, https://doi.org/10.1093/ije/dyw319.

T. Colin Campbell, Thomas M. Campbell II. 2016. *The China Study: Revised and Expanded Edition: The Most Comprehensive Study of Nutrition Ever Conducted and the Startling Implications for Diet, Weight Loss, and Long-Term Health.* Dallas: BenBella Books.

[140] Tian, Fan, Qing Shen, Yihan Hu, Weimin Ye, Unnur A. Valdimarsdóttir, Huan Song. 2022. "Association of stress-related disorders with subsequent risk of all-cause and cause-specific mortality: A population-based and sibling-controlled cohort study." *The Lancet Regional Health - Europe* Volume 18, July, 100402.

Yanek, Lisa R., Brian G. Kral, Taryn F. Moy, Dhananjay Vaidya, Mariana Lazo, Lewis C. Becker, Diane M. Becker. 2013. "Effect of Positive Well-Being on Incidence of Symptomatic Coronary Artery Disease." *Preventive Cardiology* Volume 112, Issue 8, 1120-1125, July 01, DOI:https://doi.org/10.1016/j.amjcard.2013.05.055 .

Lyubomirsky, Sonja, Laura King, Ed Diener. 2005. "The Benefits of Frequent Positive Affect: Does Happiness Lead to Success?" *American Psychological Association Psychological Bulletin* Vol. 131, No. 6, 803–855 DOI: 10.1037/0033-2909.131.6.803.

Mayo Clinic Staff. 2022. "Positive thinking: Stop negative self-talk to reduce stress." *Mayo Clinic.* February 3. Accessed February 17, 2023. https://www.mayoclinic.org/healthy-lifestyle/stress-management/in-depth/positive-thinking/art-20043950.

[141] Montez, Debra Umberson, Jennifer Karas. 2010. "Social Relationships and Health: A Flashpoint for Health Policy." *Journal of Health and Social Behavior* 51(1_suppl), S54–S66. https://doi.org/10.1177/0022146510383501 .

[142] Mueller, Paul S., David J. Plevak, Teresa A. Rummans. 2001. "Religious Involvement, Spirituality, and Medicine." *Mayo Clinic Proceedings.* "Religious Involvement, Spirituality, and Medicine." December, Vol 76.

[143] Cohen, Randy, Chirag Bavishi, Alan Rozanski. 2016. "Purpose in Life and Its Relationship to All-Cause Mortality and Cardiovascular Events Systematic review/meta-analysis." *Psychosomatic Medicine* 78(2):122-133, February/March | DOI: 10.1097/PSY.0000000000000274.

[144] Buettner, Dan. 2010. *The Blue Zones: Lessons for Living Longer From the People Who've Lived the Longest.* Washington, DC: National Geographic.

[145] Onishi, Norimitsu. 2004. "Health and Fitness: Love of U.S. food shortening Okinawans' lives / Life expectancy among islands' young men takes a big dive." *SFGate.* April 4. Accessed February 16, 2023. https://www.sfgate.com/health/article/Love-of-U-S-food-shortening-Okinawans-lives-2397590.php.

[146] Eisenberg, Richard. 2019. "Blue Zones: How The World's Oldest People Make Their Money Last." *Forbes.* April 2. Accessed February 17, 2023. https://www.forbes.com/sites/nextavenue/2019/04/02/blue-zones-how-the-worlds-oldest-people-make-their-money-last/?sh=7153c588694c.

147 Rowling, J.K. 1999. *Harry Potter and the Prisoner of Azkaban*. New York: Scholastic.

148 Khan Academy. n.d. *Lesson summary: Scarcity, choice, and opportunity costs*. Accessed February 6, 2023. https://www.khanacademy.org/economics-finance-domain/microeconomics/basic-economic-concepts-gen-micro/economics-introduction/a/lesson-overview-scarcity-choice-and-opportunity-cost#:~:text=There%20are%20four%20economic%20resources,sometimes%20referred%20to.

149 Bowers, Clint A., Deborah C. Beidel, Madeline R. Marks, Kristin Horan, Janis Cannon-Bowers. 2022. *Mental Health and Wellness in Healthcare Workers: Identifying Risks, Prevention, and Treatment (Advances in Psychology, Mental Health, and Behavioral Studies)*. Medical Information Science Reference.

150 McCann, Renetta. 2012. "Personal Resources Training: A New Approach for Building Sustainable Competitive Advantage." *Northwestern School of Education and Social Policy*. June. Accessed February 6, 2023. https://www.sesp.northwestern.edu/masters-learning-and-organizational-change/knowledge-lens/stories/2012/personal-resources-training-a-new-approach-for-building-sustainable-competitive-advantage.html. Chen, I-Shuo, Martin R Fellenz. 2020. "Personal resources and personal demands for work engagement: Evidence from employees in the service industry." *International journal of hospitality management* vol. 90: 102600. doi:10.1016/j.ijhm.2020.102600.

151 Weiss-Tisman, Howard. 2015. "Frugal benefactor leaves millions to Brattleboro Memorial Hospital and Brooks Memorial Library." *Brattleboro Reformer*. April 25. Accessed February 6, 2023. https://www.reformer.com/local-news/frugal-benefactor-leaves-millions-to-brattleboro-memorial-hospital-and-brooks-memorial-library/article_f87f8b0e-56ad-59a2-8538-549dff5d453b.html.

152 Gafoot, K. Abdul, Abidha Kurukkan. 2015. "Why High School Students Feel Mathematics is Difficult." *National Seminar on Pedagogy of Teacher Education- Trends and Challenges*.

153 Waldinger, Robert, Marc Schulz. 2023. *The Good Life: Lessons from the World's Longest Scientific Study of Happiness*. New York: Simon & Schuster.

# INDEX

# KEYNOTE SPEAKER
# AND WORKSHOP PRESENTER

Matt Paradise is a financial capability expert, but that's not all. For over twenty years, he has inspired, motivated, and guided professionals to reach seemingly impossible goals. His rich life experiences and expert knowledge are guaranteed to help your audience, business, or group achieve the success they desire.

With Matt as your keynote speaker or workshop presenter, your event is guaranteed to be motivating, entertaining, and impactful.

For more information,
visit www.MattParadise.com/speaking.

Here's what others say about Matt Paradise's presentations:

"Matt makes things better than they should be, breathing life into vision, injecting innovation into project ideas, and adding special touches on implementation that take the outcomes a mile farther than anyone thought they could go."

—NIKA ELUGARDO, Massachusetts State Representative

"The training was a nice balance of discussing larger ideas on this topic of financial education (my manager especially enjoyed hearing you address her question about disparities in communities of color and predatory practices targeted toward those communities, which affect our students) and hands-on preparation."

—KATIE CHUNG, LICSW, Massachusetts General Hospital

"Matt has such a passion for financial literacy. He has such an ability to teach to diverse populations and really can tailor his lessons and knowledge to any skill level. He is an absolute professional, has an impeccable work ethic, and builds rapport fast. It was a pleasure having him teach our young adults."

—ALYSON WHALEN, Regional Director
at Massachusetts Department of Youth Services

"Matt's commitment to providing broad access to financial education and opportunities to build assets and credit has few equals. He is an excellent communicator with a gift for connecting with others."

—PAUL HORWITZ, Retired Community Affairs Specialist, FDIC

## ABOUT THE AUTHOR

# MATT PARADISE

Matt Paradise is a renowned financial educator who is passionate about transforming lives. He has empowered more than 100,000 people to improve their credit scores, pay off their debt, and save enough money to achieve their financial goals.

As a highly sought-after speaker, he has taught people in all walks of life, from Harvard University's lecture halls to homeless shelters throughout New England. His unique programs have been featured in the Massachusetts State House, Fidelity Investments, the Department of Corrections, many nonprofits, and corporations large and small.

His leadership helped establish the Massachusetts Financial Education Collaborative, a statewide financial literacy office that created K–12 financial education legislation signed into law by Governor Charlie Baker. Matt also coauthored publications with the Massachusetts State Treasurer, the Federal Reserve Bank, and the Federal Deposit Insurance Corporation.

Matt has provided expert commentary for many media outlets, including Fox, New England Cable News (NECN), NBCUniversal, *Wall Street Watchdog*, *Street Insider*, *Telegram & Gazette*, *Benzinga*, *Credit Union Insight*, and *Credit Union Today*.

He has earned multiple licenses and certifications in the financial education field, including the Association for Financial Counseling & Planning Education (AFCPE©) Accredited Credit Counselor, Certified Educator in Personal Finance

(CEPF©), and Certified Identity Theft Risk Management Specialist (CITRMS©). Much like famed investor Warren Buffett, Matt believes that his Dale Carnegie graduation certificates are treasured investments.

Matt helped establish credit counseling and financial education departments with American Consumer Credit Counseling, which grew to support approximately 140 employees with an annual revenue in excess of $14 million. He is now an active board member leading the organization to greater growth.

A man of great faith, Matt has volunteered with multiple nonprofit boards. He served as chairman of Early Childhood Alliance, president of the Massachusetts Jump$tart Coalition, and member of the board of Boston Career Connections. Matt also ran a HOPE worldwide food pantry with his wife, serving 500 families per month. He is currently the treasurer of the MetroWest Nonprofit Network.

On his personal path to financial well-being, he has overcome drug addiction, homelessness, cancer, and a liver transplant. He is a proud father, loving husband, and care provider for his in-laws. His poodle, Odyssey, keeps him active, and music soothes his soul. He gave up a professional drumming career years ago, but enjoys playing in his church band and with friends. Matt and his family live in the Greater Boston area.

Contact Matt, book him as a speaker, and access more resources from this book at www.MattParadise.com.

Made in the USA
Middletown, DE
28 May 2023

31251630R00170